The Portuguese Empire

A Captivating Guide to the History of Portugal as a Colonial Power and Its Colonies in Asia, North and South America, and Oceania

Free Bonus from Captivating History (Available for a Limited time)

Hi History Lovers!

Now you have a chance to join our exclusive history list so you can get your first history ebook for free as well as discounts and a potential to get more history books for free! Simply visit the link below to join.

Captivatinghistory.com/ebook

Also, make sure to follow us on Facebook, Twitter and Youtube by searching for Captivating History.

Contents

Introduction: Pre-Imperial Portugal in Brief

The Portuguese are known for their feats of exploration during the so-called "Age of Discovery." The Iberian Peninsula, which is divided between Spain and Portugal, became the launching pad for European exploration.

But before we make any attempt to understand the nature of the Portuguese Empire, it would be wise to become a little better acquainted with Portugal itself. It's important to understand the founding of the Portuguese nation and what led to its sudden rise as a maritime empire. It is also important to note that, as is the case with many other regions around the world, the Portuguese people long predate the actual Portuguese state.

The first people groups of Portugal settled the land thousands of years ago. These proto-Portuguese farmed, raised animals, and left behind elaborate burial sites for their dead. When the Romans came on the scene, they called the place "Portus Cale." The land of modern-day Portugal, along with the rest of the Iberian Peninsula, was made part of the Roman Republic and, ultimately, the Roman Empire.

As a result, the local residents of what was then Portugal became thoroughly Romanized themselves. They adopted the Latin script for their language and Roman customs for their daily routines. They also developed Roman legal systems and forms of governance that would last, in some sense, long after the Roman Empire itself was torn down. During the Roman period, Portugal also developed many of its natural resources. Marble was regularly excavated, and gold, copper, and iron were in high demand.

The Roman period in Portugal came to an end roughly around the same time that the rest of the Western Roman Empire steadily fell apart at the seams, from 395 to 476 CE. It was during this span of time that Germanic tribes began to descend upon the western Romans.

The Germans came, and they conquered. But in many ways, they adopted the same Roman systems of those they had conquered. The Germanic interlopers even tried to imitate the Roman forms of monetary exchange, minting coins just like the Romans did. But perhaps most important for the future of Portugal, the Germans adopted Roman Christianity, and they enforced it during their rule.

These Christian foundations proved to be rather sturdy, and they were tested when the Iberian Peninsula was overrun by Islamic forces around 700 CE. Islamic powers would control Portugal and much of Spain for the next few centuries, but nevertheless, Christianity would remain strong even under Muslim rule. The Muslim armies first began clashing with the Germanic rulers of the Iberian Peninsula—the Visigoths—in 710.

These Muslim armies, which were based out of North Africa, were able to easily cross the narrow channel that separates the tip of Spain from the African continent. Once the armies arrived, the Germanic defenders, which at that time consisted primarily of Visigoths, found themselves hopelessly outnumbered and outmatched. And in 711, the last Germanic ruler of Iberia—King Roderic—was defeated and killed.

Although they arrived as conquerors, the subsequent Islamic governance of Spain and Portugal is said to have been generally tolerant. The Muslim overlords of Spain proved to be fairly benevolent and accepting of those under their dominion. They did indeed build mosques and encouraged conversion to Islam, but they did not interfere with the Christianity that was already in place. They were also tolerant of Jewish residents, allowing them to practice and live life as they pleased.

The Islamic governance of Portugal also brought an advanced culture and technological innovations—some of it borrowed from the Greeks—that western Europe was still not aware of. Their expertise in shipbuilding, compasses, and astrolabes, in particular, would become of immense importance during the later rise of the Portuguese Empire. The Portuguese borrowed these ideas from the Muslims, and it would eventually make them the masters of the high seas.

Nevertheless, the Muslims who had brought such knowledge were themselves driven out at the start of the so-called "Reconquista" of the Iberian Peninsula. Just like the Crusades, which sought to bring the conquered Holy Land back into Christian hands, the Christians of Europe sought to recapture or re-conquer the Iberian Peninsula as well. Although the crusading Christians would have a toehold in the Holy Land for a while (from 1098 to 1291), their efforts would ultimately prove much more successful and longer lasting in Portugal and Spain.

After all, in the centuries since the Reconquista, Portugal and Spain (at least as of this writing) have not been retaken as part of an Islamic caliphate. And Portugal was ripped from Muslim hands as early as 868 when a large portion of the region that today constitutes modern-day Portugal was taken by the Christians. It was named simply the "County of Portugal."

The commander who led the successful taking of this land was Vimara Peres, who would subsequently be handed leadership of the territory. The County of Portugal continued to gain strength, and by the late 900s, the leadership was in the habit of referring to themselves as the "Grand Duke of Portugal." However, the County of Portugal faced an unforeseen threat when Vikings from the far north dropped down on the unsuspecting Portuguese in 968.

After surviving this assault, the County of Portugal became more closely connected with the Kingdom of León. The Kingdom of León had been founded as an autonomous Christian kingdom carved out of a northwestern chunk of the Iberian Peninsula in 910. In time, the County of Portugal would eventually become entirely independent, transforming into the Kingdom of Portugal in 1139.

This independence was confirmed by none other than the pope. In 1179, Pope Alexander III issued an official papal bull called *Manifestis Probatum*, in which Portugal's autonomous nature was officially recognized. The pope established that Afonso Henriques (r. 1139–1185) was the first official king of Portugal. The Portuguese Empire would ultimately be built upon the foundations of this kingdom.

An overall look at how large the Portuguese Empire was. The lines in the ocean show the Portuguese spice trade routes to Asia. The larger squares show their major factories.

Chapter 1 – Portugal Discovers the World

"I am not the man I once was. I do not want to go back in time; to be the second son—the second man."

-Vasco da Gama

If you have ever heard it said that a particular nation has discovered something, such phrases are usually a bit of a misnomer. Most of the time, those discoveries had already been discovered by someone else. For example, for a long time, people said that Christopher Columbus "discovered" America. The Americas, however, had already been discovered by the Vikings, and they had long been inhabited by various Native tribes.

In consideration of such things, it makes the claim of this discovery seem rather narrow-minded. Christopher Columbus and his men may have discovered something they themselves (as well as most of the known world) did not know existed, but that does not mean that others were not already well aware of it. In much the same way, the so-called "Age of Discovery," of which Portugal was a part, must be looked at with this same lens.

The Portuguese, who had long been locked in dynastic struggles, finally stabilized their society enough to leave their home base and discover the world. Not so much for others but for themselves. The earliest of these Portuguese expeditions seems to have kicked off around 1415 CE. During this fateful year, the Portuguese executed their conquest of Ceuta.

Ceuta was an important city and an outpost situated in an Islamic caliphate located in modern-day Morocco. Ceuta was actually the launching-off point for much of the original Islamic conquest of the Iberian Peninsula back in the 700s. Just a short distance from Spain, the city of Ceuta had long been an Islamic stronghold. The fact that the Portuguese were able to go on the offensive against the very city that had staged the conquest of the Iberian Peninsula centuries before was of symbolic as well as strategic importance.

Ceuta was strategically important because it resided on the other side of the famed Straits of Gibraltar, allowing better control over the commerce that traversed through this narrow channel of water. The conquest of Ceuta was led by none other than King John of Portugal (r. 1385–1433). King John led a strike force, which landed off the coast of Playa San Amara and managed to catch Ceuta's defenders completely off-guard. King John's invasion force consisted of some forty-five thousand troops, and they were backed up by some two hundred naval craft, which parked just offshore. This was a bit overkill, but it is a clear indication that King John was not willing to take any chances.

At any rate, the town was quickly subdued, and it fell into the hands of the Portuguese forces by the following morning. Although the taking of Ceuta may seem minor at first glance, it marks the beginning of Portuguese imperial expansion. The Christian kingdoms of Portugal and Spain had been on the defensive against Muslim encroachment for centuries. But now, with the Reconquista of the Iberian Peninsula just about complete, the Portuguese were actually going on the offensive by directly taking over territory in North Africa, which had long been dominated by Muslim powers.

Building on these gains, in 1419, the Portuguese made their first inroads in Macaronesia—an island chain located just to the northwest of the African continent. Around the year 1419, they had subdued Madeira, an island that they would eventually make rich in sugarcane. The Portuguese then reached into the Azores by 1427, thereby ensuring their foothold in Macaronesia. Initially, the main thrust of this Portuguese expansion was to dominate the sea routes and enhance trade, although colonization for the sake of settlements would come in time.

The real goal of the Portuguese during this period was the circumnavigation of the African continent. Such a feat would allow them to bypass the traditional land routes to East Asia. After the fall of the Byzantine Empire in 1453 to the Ottoman Empire and the subsequent Muslim domination of the former land routes that ran through it, the search for a sea route to the east became all the more imperative. So, the Portuguese continued to advance down the coasts of Africa. In 1456, Portugal obtained yet another coastal acquisition when they seized Cape Verde.

They continued to progress southwest down the African coastline. By the 1460s, the Portuguese had moved into the Gulf of Guinea, which is located right along the equator, roughly at the mid-section of the African continent. The Portuguese set up shop on islands in the gulf, such as São Tomé and Príncipe. Here, they found traces of gold and other minerals.

However, the Portuguese were not the only ones vying for a spot in the Gulf of Guinea. The Kingdom of Castile had sent explorers to the region as well. The Portuguese and the Castilians would continue to butt heads, leading to the breakout of the Battle of Guinea in 1478. In a similar way to the taking of Ceuta decades prior, the Portuguese launched an overwhelming surprise naval attack on the Castilians. The Castilians were caught completely unaware, and their ships were literally blown to pieces in some cases. The ships that were not destroyed ended up in Portuguese hands, along with a considerable amount of gold, which was handed over when the Castilians were forced to give up the fight.

The Portuguese would ultimately prevail in this struggle, securing their complete domination of the Gulf of Guinea. Ensuring their monopoly, the Portuguese built the outpost of São Jorge da Mina, situated on what today comprises the coast of Ghana. The Portuguese had continued their expansive exploration in the meantime, having ventured south of the equator for the first time in 1473 and then making inroads into the Congo River by 1482.

In the following year, 1483, the Portuguese explorers would push even farther south, reaching what we now call Angola. Once ashore, in dramatic fashion, the Portuguese explorers laid claim to the land by placing a large stone monument the Portuguese called a *padrão* on the shore. The monument had an inscription that read, "In the era of 6681 years from the creation of the world, 1482 years since the birth of Our Lord Jesus, the Most High and Excellent and Mighty Prince, King D. Joao [sometimes rendered John] II of Portugal, sent Diogo Cao squire of his House to discover this land and plant these pillars."

These supposed discoveries and claims were made no matter what the previous inhabitants of the newly "discovered" lands might have thought about it. In fact, this was quite common throughout the whole Age of Discovery. But this monument was more than an attempt to stake out future territory. It was meant to serve as a marker of just how far the Portuguese had traveled up to that point in their quest to circumnavigate Africa.

A drawing by Alfredo Roque Gameiro of the erection of a padrão at the mouth of the Zaire River.

As evidence of how meticulously planned each leg of these exploratory missions was, this particular plaque had been carved several months prior to the launching of the mission. Thus, even though the actual placement of the monument was in 1483, it was inscribed with 1482—the date it was first carved back in Portugal.

In consideration of what was at stake and the resources expended, these expeditions by the Portuguese have been likened to the Apollo moon missions during the 1960s. And such comparisons would not be too far off the mark. For just like the Apollo missions to land on the moon, these efforts by Portugal took considerable sums of money, both in regards to their organization and their execution. Like the moon missions, they also took Portuguese explorers into what was then entirely unknown territory.

No outsiders had been this far down the African coast. Even Arab explorers who had long been a presence in North Africa had not sailed down the coast of West Africa like this. Much like the fears expressed by European sailors about crossing the Atlantic, Arab sailors often spoke of terrible consequences that were in store for anyone who sailed through the uncharted waters down the west coast of Africa and around the continent's southern tip.

Yet, despite such fears, the Portuguese pushed on. And they made an important discovery during these voyages. They found that although the howling winds near the shores of the African coast were often treacherous and deadly, if they just sailed a little farther west into the equatorial Atlantic, they could rely upon strong westerly winds to launch them back on course to Portugal.

This slingshot effect proved to be so helpful that it soon became a major part of their journey around Africa's southern tip. They would hug the African coast all the way to the equator, and once they reached that area, they would sail off to the west and use the strong winds to launch themselves rapidly southeast. Eventually, they made it around the southern tip of Africa. It was a moment of pure genius, and it would change the world.

Chapter 2 – The Search for India

"Each ship had three sets of sails and anchors and three or four times as much other tackle and rigging as was usual. The cooperage of the casks, pipes and barrels for wine, water vinegar and oil was strengthened with many hoops of iron. The provisions of bread, wine, flour, meat vegetables, medicines, and likewise of arms and ammunition, were also in excess of what was needed for such a voyage. The best and most skillful pilots and mariners in Portugal were sent on this voyage, and they received, besides other favors, salaries higher than those of any seamen of other countries. The money spent on the few ships of this expedition was so great that I will not go into detail for fear of not being believed."

-Duarte Pacheco Pereira

In the spring of 1488, the Portuguese first managed to sail right past the tip of southern Africa. This event dispelled the long-held belief that the Indian Ocean was "land-locked." It would be realized that by rounding the tip of Africa, one could very well make their way to the Indian Ocean and ultimately to India itself.

This expedition was led by the daring Portuguese explorer Bartolomeu Dias, who had first left on this epic voyage the previous year, sailing out of Lisbon, Portugal, in 1487. Bartolomeu Dias and his crew then reached the tip of Africa in 1488, and despite any misgivings they may have had, they successfully navigated their way around it.

However, at the time, they were unsure of exactly where they were and of how far they could go in these uncharted waters. After rounding the tip of Africa, the Portuguese sailed north along the eastern shores of the African continent. They stopped at a few places on the coast, where they noticed some native inhabitants who stared in shock at the strange ships and visitors that confronted them.

It has been said that at one point, Dias and his crew stopped to take in some water a little inland but were ambushed by some locals. Fortunately for Dias and his companions, it seemed that all their antagonists were equipped with were rocks, as they showered them with rock-like projectiles. According to the Portuguese account of what happened next, Dias took out the powerfully built Portuguese crossbow he had with him and launched an arrow at his attackers.

As a result, one was killed, and the rest fled from the scene—no doubt telling others to be wary of these strange intruders. The Portuguese then returned to their ships and resumed their journey up Africa's eastern coast. Soon, they noticed that the waters, which had cooled considerably as they rounded the southern tip, were getting warmer, indicating a return toward the equator. The crew wanted to proceed farther, but their supplies were dangerously low.

Thus, they stopped on March 12th, took a brief rest, and took the time to plant yet another monument as a mile marker. The location they had reached was situated in the Eastern Cape province, near the town of Kwaaihoek. The marker still stands to this day, and it serves as a popular tourist attraction. After they placed this marker, the crew then went back to their ships and began their fateful journey back south, back around the African continent and—or so they hoped— home to Portugal.

It was around this time that another Portuguese explorer by the name of Pêro (Pedro) da Covhilã was making an extraordinary journey of his own. Covhilã was in search of the fabled Prester John of Africa. For centuries, it had been rumored in Christian Europe that there was a great and powerful Christian monarch located somewhere beyond the Muslim-dominated lands of North Africa and the Middle East. Some tales hinted that he was in Asia, while others hinted that he was somewhere in Africa. It was believed that this isolated but powerful Christian kingdom would be a tremendous ally in the struggle of the Christian powers against Islam.

Interestingly enough, there was indeed a powerful (although perhaps not as powerful as the rumors suggested) and thriving Christian kingdom in East Africa that the larger Christian world knew practically nothing about. We are talking about the Christian Ethiopian Empire. The Ethiopian Empire had been around since 1270, and it was one of the very first countries to officially adopt Christianity, doing so in the 4th century under the Kingdom of Aksum.

Initially, Ethiopia had solid relations with other neighboring regions that had also turned to Christianity. After Islam swept through what had previously been a Christian-based North Africa around 700 CE, Ethiopia suddenly found itself cut off from the rest of the Christian world.

So, just like the myth of Prester John suggested, there was indeed an isolated but thriving Christian kingdom cut off from the rest of Christendom, south of the Islamic bloc. Covhilã was in search of this long-sought-after realm, but he didn't take a powerful armada of ships around the tip of Africa to find it. Instead, he simply disguised himself and quietly traversed the treacherous overland routes, journeying through the Holy Land, Saudi Arabia, and into the Horn of Africa.

From here, he proceeded to the Ethiopian Empire, where he was cordially greeted by Ethiopian Emperor Eskender. But although he was treated well enough, Eskender actually forbade Covhilã from leaving his realm. He essentially kept Covhilã as a highly pampered prisoner in his kingdom. Such things seem to only add to the mystique of medieval Ethiopia since so many legends of mythical realms speak of intrepid explorers entering paradises but never returning.

In Eskender's royal court, Covhilā was treated as a guest of honor. He was given all he ever wanted, except for one thing—a way to return home. But as mysterious as such actions might seem, there are a few reasons why the Ethiopian monarch may have acted in this manner. In those days, Ethiopia was very secretive and deeply concerned about potential intrusions from outsiders. And one can hardly blame them, considering how much outside powers ended up exploiting so many African kingdoms.

In many ways, Ethiopia's best defense from outside manipulation was its sheer remoteness. Ethiopia was hard to find—and the ruling powers thought it prudent to keep it that way. Although Covhilā was not allowed to leave, he was indeed treated with great distinction. He was made a member of the king's court and eventually married an Ethiopian woman, with whom he raised a family. Covhilā would ultimately die, with his Ethiopian friends and family members at his side, in 1526.

Nevertheless, the friendship that had been forged between Portugal and Ethiopia would prove pivotal for the latter. In the following year, 1527, a Muslim power rose up in eastern Ethiopia. A military leader by the name of Ahmad ibn Ibrahim al-Ghazi cobbled together an army that threatened the entirety of the Christian Ethiopian Empire. The struggle would go on for decades. By the 1530s, Ethiopian Emperor Lebna-Dengel (also known as Dawit II; Dengel is an Amharic variation of David, as in King David of the Bible) was throwing the full might of his army against the Islamic forces, but his enemy continued to gain the upper hand.

The emperor himself ultimately fell in battle but not before sending off an urgent request for military aid to the Portuguese. These entreaties would lead to the Portuguese intervening in the conflict in 1540. Portugal only sent four hundred troops, but they were equipped with the latest weaponry. These hardened Portuguese fighters were enough to tip the scales in favor of the Ethiopians. At the Battle of Wayna Daga in 1543, the Muslim forces of Ahmad ibn Ibrahim were finally defeated, with Ahmad being one of the casualties.

The assistance of the Portuguese no doubt helped to ensure that the only indigenous Christian nation left in Africa was allowed to remain standing. It is somewhat ironic that for centuries, the Christians of Europe whispered about a powerful Christian king of the East—Prester John—hidden somewhere behind the Muslim forces. The tales often spoke of how this great Christian king would rise up to aid the Christians of Europe during their darkest hour.

In reality, though, it was the Christians of Europe who ended up aiding Christian Ethiopia in its darkest hour. Say what you will about the Portuguese and some of their later exploitations of the natives, but if they had not ventured to Ethiopia in the 1540s, the empire might well have been conquered by Muslim forces. Although forced conversion goes against Islamic law, the Muslims still placed an exorbitant tax on those who did not convert. If one could not pay this tax, a person could be sentenced to death, exiled, or forcibly converted. (Typically, they were more lenient to those who practiced Judaism and Christianity, although the tax still applied to them.) The Portuguese arriving when they did turned out to be a miracle for the continuity of the Ethiopian civilization and the longevity of its long Christian heritage.

But we are getting ahead of ourselves in the discussion of the general chronological progression of the Portuguese Empire. Putting aside these events of the 1500s, let us transport ourselves back to the 1480s when both Pêro da Covhilã's overland journey and Bartolomeu Dias's sea journey were still under way. This decade was a pivotal one for Portugal. Columbus had yet to discover the New World for Spain, so the Portuguese were the ones making most of the major discoveries.

That fateful 1492 voyage of Columbus was, of course, mainly launched to search for a new route to India. Ever since the fall of

Constantinople to the Ottoman Empire in 1453, overland routes to the Far East had been cut off. This event was what first led the heads of state in Europe to contemplate the discovery of a new route via the high seas. And as a lasting hallmark of his true intentions, Christopher Columbus was Genoese (some believe he might have been Portuguese, Spanish, or even Polish; as of this writing, genetic testing is being conducted on his remains), but he sailed for the Spanish Crown. Upon landing in the Americas (more precisely, the Bahamas) in 1492, he called the native inhabitants Indians.

This, of course, reflects what his prime directive was. The goal was not to discover the Americas but to find an alternative route to India. And Columbus sincerely believed he was in India at the time. He had sailed west across the Atlantic in the hopes of finding the backdoor to India. Little did he know that there was a whole continent in his way. The Portuguese, on the other hand, were working on a route that would take them south around the tip of Africa and up to India. And they were quite confident that they would be able to do it.

In fact, they were so confident that in 1485, some three years prior to Dias's circumnavigation of Africa, King John (João) II of Portugal was openly bragging to the pope that his explorers would soon be sailing to India. In 1488, however, Bartolomeu Dias's expedition did not make it to India. He ultimately had to turn back before reaching the Indian subcontinent. But his journey around the southern tip of Africa paved the way for future expeditions to follow in his footsteps.

The political happenings in Portugal proper would postpone these follow-up trips. On July 13th, 1491, for example, King John II's presumptive heir to the throne—Prince Afonso—abruptly perished from a horse-riding accident. This set Portugal up for a succession crisis. Figuring out who would be next in line to King John II became absolutely paramount.

It was soon determined that the crown would go to "Manuel, Duke of Beja. King John II actually had a son born out of wedlock named Dom Jorge, whom he wished to pass his throne to, but when it was clear that such a thing would never be seen as legitimate, he finally settled on his cousin, Manuel, instead. King John II ultimately perished in 1495, and the reins of power were officially handed over to Manuel.

King John II was only forty years of age when he passed. The fact that the king died so early in his reign bears testament to the importance of having a successor. Fortunately for Portugal, Manuel was ready to take on the burden of leadership as soon as King John II passed. There are those, of course, who have suggested that perhaps King John II's demise was not a natural one and that he was poisoned to hasten the succession of Manuel to the throne.

But besides whispered rumors, there is no evidence that this was the case.

King John II's death seemed to have taken most people by surprise. He was at the height of his power, and in the previous year of 1494, he had overseen the forging of the famed Treaty of Tordesillas, which basically divided all of the new territories beyond Europe's frontiers between the Portuguese and the Spanish.

Ever since Christopher Columbus led Spain into the Americas in 1492, it was clear that Spain would be Portugal's main competitor in the search for new land. The 1494 Treaty of Tordesillas, which was sanctioned by none other than the pope, sought to avoid any future friction by having these two Catholic powers agree ahead of time on who would claim what. This treaty essentially divided the spoils of newly found territories between the two, with the arbitrarily created Tordesillas line situated some 370 leagues west of the Portuguese-controlled Azores. Spain had access to the territory west of the line, and Portugal had access to the territory east of it.

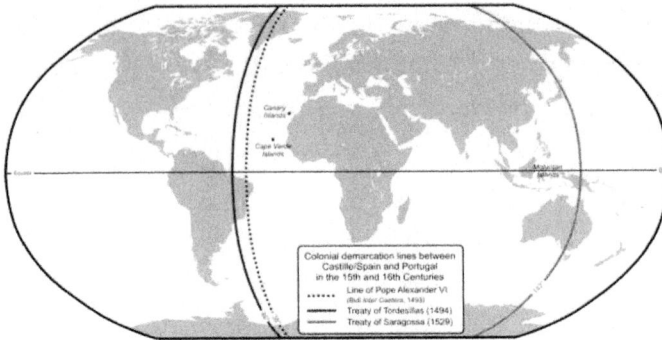

The lines of the Treaty of Tordesillas and the later Treaty of Zaragoza (Saragossa).

It is amazing that Portugal and Spain could agree to such things diplomatically and without coming to blows over who controlled what piece of colonial real estate. Disputes would indeed arise many years later, but for quite some time, both parties would abide by this ruling.

It has been suggested that the final hammering out of these terms during the last days of Portugal's King John II, combined with the uncertainty of the succession of the new king, Manuel I, in 1495, were all factors that delayed the next major Portuguese expedition. It was not until two years after Manual took the throne that the famed navigator Vasco da Gama disembarked from Portugal. Vasco da Gama would not only follow in the path laid by Bartolomeu Dias in 1488 when he rounded the southern tip of Africa; Vasco da Gama would push even farther. He would end up finding the greatest prize of all—a route to India itself.

Chapter 3 – The Journey of Vasco da Gama

"I am not afraid of the darkness. Real death is preferable to a life without living."

-Vasco da Gama

The soon-to-be-famous explorer Vasco da Gama sailed out of a Portuguese port in the summer of 1497. In his possession were two letters. One was made out to Prester John, who was now believed to be the emperor of Ethiopia. And the other was meant for the Raja or ruler of the region of southern India known as Calicut. Portuguese intelligence had long found out that Calicut was a major hub in the Indian spice trade. And since this was a major industry that the Portuguese wished to become involved with, it was only natural that they would go to its source.

It has long been said that the voyages of discovery, both to the Americas and India, have revolved around the search for spices. In modern times, it might be hard for us to understand why it seemed so imperative for Europeans to find new ways to access something as seemingly trivial as pepper, nutmeg, ginger, cinnamon, cloves, and the like. But these things must be taken into perspective.

Indian spices played a major role in the economies of countries at the time. Spices were a much sought-after yet rare commodity due to the distance of Indian ports from most of their would-be customers. And ever since the fall of Constantinople in 1453, Arab armies blocked the route by land. Arab merchants had largely become the middlemen, which only served to ratchet up the price that European merchants paid to acquire these goods.

The monopoly that these traders had over spices would be akin to one group of people having an iron grip on something as crucial for modern-day life today, such as microprocessors. The world is run on computers, and computers need microprocessors. In the 1400s and 1500s, Indian spices were seen as an incredibly valuable commodity.

Let us delve deeper into our modern-day example. As of this writing, Taiwan makes more of these microprocessors than anyone else. Taiwan is currently able to trade openly with the world, and there isn't much of a problem with the status quo of this arrangement. However, China considers Taiwan a part of its territory and would like to reclaim it. If China were to suddenly seize the independent republic of Taiwan by force, China would then have a complete monopoly on microprocessors. Such a thing would be akin to the fall of Constantinople. Such a development would have a significant impact on the global economy since the world would depend on China for much-needed computer chips. If it really did come to this, then it could be argued that it would take a modern-day Vasco da Gama to break up this monopoly by somehow wresting control of this commodity back from the Chinese.

At any rate, moving on from our example, the very same sort of geopolitical stakes was at work during Vasco da Gama's voyage in 1497. The trek was not made merely because some Europeans desperately needed access to spices to liven up their food—it was to break up a monopoly that was crippling much of the European economy. And da Gama would be ultimately successful in that task.

Along with his letters of introduction, Vasco da Gama's crew was also equipped with various real-life sample products of the things he wished to gain during the trip. He had samples of gold, seed pearls, and, of course, the much-coveted spices. If Vasco da Gama and his explorers encountered a language barrier, these products would be used as visual aids to help them communicate what they wanted with the local inhabitants.

Just imagine Vasco da Gama pulling up at a port in India and showing the curious locals samples of spices. Just by sight, they would know what Vasco da Gama and his crew were after, and they would be able to lead them to the right people to begin the necessary transactions to get them.

The first leg of this epic voyage had Vasco da Gama and company heading southwest from Portugal. About a week into the trip, the explorers reached the Canary Islands. By the end of July, they had passed the Cape Verde Islands. After they were about seven hundred miles south of the Cape Verde Islands, Vasco da Gama's ships did what, at that time, was still quite unexpected. They all headed west and sailed to the mid-point of the Atlantic before utilizing the westerly winds to send them sailing right toward the tip of South Africa.

Since no one on board these vessels at the time had any assurance that this tactic would send them back on course, it was a daring move. It was just about as daring as the Apollo astronauts heading out into the unknown depths of space to land on the moon. And when taken into consideration, the Portuguese explorers were actually a lot more daring since these bold sailors had no mission control to radio back to in case there was a problem. No—these Portuguese explorers were completely on their own.

They did have the example of Bartolomeu Dias's previous trek to follow, but they sailed much farther west than Dias ever did, taking full advantage of the westerly winds. The fact that they knew how to do this has led some historians to speculate that there must have been other tentative expeditions in between Dias and da Gama, but there is no clear evidence to back such theories up.

At any rate, even with the westerly winds helping to push them toward the tip of Africa, it still took several more days to round it due to the ships being battered with stormy winds. Upon rounding the tip of Africa, the ships made a pit stop on the east side of Africa's tip. Here, they rested and made contact with some of the locals. This contact was noted by one of the expedition's crew members, who took note of how the local residents greeted them.

Our anonymous man wrote, "They brought with them about a dozen oxen and cows and flour or five sheep. As soon as we saw them we went ashore. They forthwith began to play on four or five flutes, some producing high notes and other low ones." The man then went on to state, "The captain-major then ordered the trumpets to be sounded, and we, in the boats, danced, and the captain-major did so likewise when he rejoined us."

It was not always this easygoing for these intrepid explorers, however. By mid-December, the crew had reached the point where Bartolomeu Dias had stopped his own expedition in 1488 to turn back for Portugal. Instead of turning back, Vasco da Gama and his crew braved the stormy winds that battered the coasts of southeastern Africa and pushed farther north up the African coast. In early January of 1498, ten years after Dias's fateful decision to turn back, these explorers found themselves in what to them was a brand-new land.

They immediately noticed the uniqueness of the settlements they saw along the coast. These villages were much denser, and some had impressive mosques with tall minarets. Upon making landfall, the Portuguese found that the locals were not quite as astonished as other locals had been to see them. They actually seemed to expect them, as if the arrival of faraway visitors was more or less routine.

It was soon discovered that many of the locals were part of the Bantu people. This provided a breakthrough moment for the expedition since they had interpreters on board who were familiar with the Bantu language. The crew was greeted well by the locals, and the men were able to stop, replenish their supplies, and rest a bit before moving farther north along the East African coast.

Vasco da Gama's expedition sailed north up the strait between the East African coast and the island of Madagascar in early spring, and by March, the Portuguese made their way to the famed port of Mozambique. The locals at this port spoke Arabic, and they were able to converse freely with the crew's Arabic interpreters. In this trading town, they met rich Muslim traders decked out in expensive clothing and the finest gold and jewels.

The merchants were used to receiving faraway visitors, but they were indeed curious as to where their guests were from. Initially, these Mozambique merchants assumed that the Portuguese must be Turks who had somehow discovered a new route to the east by sea. After several conversations between the locals and interpreters, the crew realized that the locals assumed they were Muslims just like them. The Portuguese quickly decided that given the hostilities between these two religions in those days that it was probably in their best interest for the merchants of Mozambique to continue operating under this assumption.

After a local sultan greeted the visitors, he asked to see examples of the Turks' famed bows and well-crafted Qurans. The crew sought to keep up the façade. Da Gama had his interpreters concoct a likely story, informing the sultan and anyone else who might happen to ask that while they were not from Turkey, they were from a country near Turkey. Perhaps by using such vague statements, these Christian explorers felt a little better about the deception.

It was certainly a gross exaggeration to suggest that Portugal was anywhere near Turkey. Portugal is thousands of miles away from Turkey. And as it pertained to their exquisite, well-crafted Qurans? These Portuguese sailors claimed that their books were far too sacred to risk damage by carrying them over the sea. As for their famous bows, the Portuguese were more than ready to brandish their best crossbows and put on a demonstration from the decks of their ships for those interested.

One of the Portuguese chroniclers wrote that their hosts were "much pleased and greatly astonished." After getting into the good graces of this local sultan, the Portuguese requested and were granted a couple of local navigators who could show them how to best traverse the Indian Ocean.

However, one of these pilots would realize what was going on with these so-called "Muslims." Just as they were preparing to make their way to India, one of the navigators realized the façade for what it was—that these Muslims were actually Christians. He made a break for it and literally jumped ship. The Portuguese tried to track the runaway pilot down, but they could not catch him.

Bad weather then arrived, and the Portuguese, along with their remaining navigator—now turned veritable hostage—were forced to remain where they were. They were in desperate need of water, and after the storm died down, they made landfall in Mozambique under cover of darkness. The next day, they ventured out to a spring to get water but found their path blocked by several local guards.

It was quite clear now that the people of Mozambique knew that the Portuguese were not who they said they were. Unable to get what they wanted from the increasingly hostile locals, the Portuguese, with their better-armed naval craft, would soon resort to an early form of gunboat diplomacy. They parked their ships near the watering hole, and if anyone came near the crew as they disembarked to get water, the ship's cannons roared to life. The Portuguese retrieved water for the last time on March 25th before heading out of Mozambique for the last time.

The next major port these intrepid explorers reached was that of Mombasa. Today, Mombasa is the second-largest city in Kenya, but back in the 1500s, Kenya as a nation did not exist. Mombasa was a thriving port city in what was then known as the Swahili coast. Mombasa played a big role in trade across the Indian Ocean, with skilled local navigators crossing back and forth between East African port cities like Mombasa and the bustling ports of India.

The Portuguese were received well at first, but after a few weeks, relations soured. One night, some local men were caught trying to sabotage the rigging on some of the ships. They had swum up to the ships while they were parked and attempted to cut the lines. The would-be saboteurs were chased off before any major damage occurred, but it was clear to the Portuguese that it was time to move on.

It was now mid-April, and the Portuguese made their way some seventy miles north, landing at the next major hub on the Swahili coast—the port city of Malindi. Malindi had long been a trading hub in the region, trading with merchants as far away as Saudi Arabia, India, and at times even China. In 1414, the famed Chinese admiral Zheng He sailed into Malindi's ports. Vasco da Gama and company were following in the footsteps of previous navigators such as these when they landed at Malindi in the spring of 1498.

It was here that the Portuguese first came into contact with Indian merchants, whom they actually mistook for the Eastern Christians that they were so desperately looking for. Shortly after their arrival, they made contact with a group of Indian merchants who they managed to erroneously project their own beliefs upon. These men were Hindu believers, yet after they were shown a painting of Jesus and Mother Mary, their reaction convinced the Portuguese that they were Christians. The men obviously sensed the reverence of the religious icons, and they bowed down in reverence and were heard shouting what the Portuguese thought to be "Christ! Christ!" Some historians have since concluded that the Indian merchants were most likely exclaiming, "Krishna! Krishna!"

It is not too hard to imagine that the Hindu believers mixed up an image of Christ with Krishna since the depictions of the two have always had some similarities. Even some of the attributes given to Krishna could be said to be similar to Christ. Little did the Portuguese know then that they could very well have been mistaking *Krishnians* for *Christians.*

At any rate, according to journals from crew members, it seems the Portuguese had a jolly time in Malindi, and the local sultan even gave them another navigator who was more than willing to lead them to India proper. On April 24th, Vasco da Gama and his ships left Malindi and headed for the Indian port of Calicut.

Their trip from the coasts of East Africa across the Indian Ocean to India would take just a few weeks, with the crew making landfall in India in late May. In far-flung India, they would find those with whom they could converse freely. Most of the Portuguese crew knew how to speak their sister language of Spanish. This would prove important because shortly after their arrival in India, they came across a couple of merchants who originally hailed from the North African nation of Tunisia, who spoke fluent Spanish.

The merchants were apparently quite surprised to see these European explorers. They were particularly amazed that they had somehow made their way to India. It has been said that Vasco da Gama sent one of his scouts, a man by the name of João Nunes, to speak with the locals. One of the first things that these Spanish-speaking merchants asked him was, "What the devil has brought you here?" To this question, João Nunes gave the now famous reply, "We have come to seek Christians and spices."

For the Spanish conquistadors of the Americas, it has long been said that their main motivations were for "God, gold, and glory!" For the Portuguese then, it could be said that the simplistic anthem they sang was for "Christians and spices!" After all, Vasco da Gama had two letters of introduction, one for the famed Christian king Prester John and another for the Raja.

Vasco da Gama hoped to cut a lucrative trade deal in exotic Indian spices with the Raja. Da Gama and a small company of his were scheduled to meet with the local Raja, known as the Samoothiri Raja, on May 28th. They had an anonymous chronicler with them who recorded parts of this momentous event. Before meeting with the Raja, they met with the Raja's subordinate governor, referred to as his *bale*. The *bale* led them to a welcoming committee at a local home, where they were given a fine meal of rice and fish. Although his companions dined in style, da Gama himself, always a bit paranoid in new and unfamiliar surroundings lest someone slip him some poison, refused to eat any of it.

After the meal came to a close, da Gama and company were directed to a couple of boats that had been joined together so that the group could travel by river to reach the Raja's palace. Once the river took them as far as it could, da Gama was placed in a palanquin. This was a kind of large box that was used as a carriage. It rested on long poles and was lifted up on the shoulders of others so that those inside could be literally carried to their destination.

Seated in his palanquin, da Gama was able to observe the crowds that had gathered along the way to watch this strange procession. Prior to reaching the palace, they stopped at what was most likely a Hindu temple, but da Gama and company, who were still quite confused about Hinduism, took it to be a church of some unknown Christian sect. Da Gama took the time to pray inside the temple before he was led back out and brought the rest of the way to the Raja's palace.

The chronicler who accompanied da Gama described the interior of the palace as being quite magnificent. He later wrote that it was "a great hall, surrounded with seats of timber raised in rows above one another like our theaters, the floor being covered by a carpet of green velvet, and the walls hung with silk of various colors." Within this grand palace, da Gama would first gain an audience to the Raja.

After the introductory greetings had been conducted, da Gama requested and was granted the opportunity to speak with the Raja in private. It was not completely done in private, of course, since interpreters were required. But the meeting was shielded from the vast majority of curious onlookers, so it was about as private of an audience as Vasco da Gama would be able to get. Da Gama proceeded to inform the Raja of the great mission he had been charged with by Manuel, King of Portugal.

He spoke at length of how his countrymen had been seeking a new route to India for some sixty years—ever since the fall of Constantinople. Along with seeking to reopen trade with India, da Gama also spoke of how he was seeking out Christian kings. It remains unclear what the Raja thought of the notion of the Portuguese seeking out "Christian kings." Much of what da Gama was saying was probably lost in translation, and the context may have been completely misunderstood.

But the Raja did understand the basics of da Gama's intention to reopen trade with India. After laying down the basics of why he had come to India, da Gama and company bid the Raja farewell and retired for the evening. As was customary, the next day, da Gama had goods unloaded from his ships to give to the Raja as presents. These goods were intercepted by the Raja's governor, who immediately considered them not to be adequate as royal presents.

The governor is said to have remarked that any gift given to the great Raja "should be in gold," not the measly brass bracelets, beads, and other cheap trinkets that the Portuguese apparently had on board. Da Gama was deeply frustrated at this turn of events, and he is said to have protested that he was "no merchant but an ambassador." He also insisted that if he were able to make a return trip, he would be sure to have "far richer presents" the second time around.

Da Gama was on a voyage of discovery; thus, he was not quite prepared to shower a local potentate with gifts. His men were lucky to have just reached India alive and with their ships in one piece. It was for this reason that da Gama promised that their gifts would be much better on a return visit since the major hurdle of simply navigating to India had been achieved.

Da Gama told the governor that he wished to have another audience with the Raja so that he could better describe the plight he was in. He was granted this audience, but he was told that he was only allowed to have two of his men accompany him. Da Gama was deeply suspicious of these developments and feared for their safety, lest they suddenly be seized and held hostage. Nevertheless, he didn't see any other option but to take the Raja up on his invitation.

The Raja was greatly confused as to why they would come to a place renowned for exotic trade goods with only mere beads and other trinkets. Da Gama once again tried to explain himself, stating that this expedition was one of "discovery." He had to explain the risk of traveling into unknown waters and how the king of Portugal was not willing to load up ships with silver and gold only for them to possibly fall off the edge of the earth (some did indeed still speculate that such a thing might happen).

In the end, it is thought that da Gama's efforts to explain the nature of his expedition managed to partially appease the great Raja. He was then given permission to have his ships unload goods at the docks and sell and trade whatever they were able to.

But this was most certainly not the end of Vasco da Gama's problems in India. After leaving the palace, he asked for small boats he could use to transfer himself to his ships, which were cautiously waiting a short distance away. The governor then made what he no doubt thought was a reasonable request, as he asked da Gama to have his ships pull in closer to shore. Da Gama, however, was intensely suspicious of his hosts. He feared that if the ships actually pulled into port, they might somehow be trapped and blocked from leaving. Da Gama's Indian hosts, on the other hand, feared that if they granted da Gama's request and paddled him all the way out to his ships that da Gama and company might simply take off without paying the customary service charge, which all visiting craft were obligated to pay.

This disagreement of how to get da Gama back onto his ships led to an incredibly uneasy situation. Da Gama became increasingly incensed at the hold-up. He told the governor that he would like to speak with the Raja once again. This was agreed to, but as would be expected in a busy kingdom such as the Raja's, it would take some time for another meeting to be arranged.

In the meantime, da Gama was kept in a local house, surrounded by armed guards. He was increasingly feeling more like a hostage than an esteemed guest. The chronicler who was still in da Gama's company at this time recorded just how incredibly dire the ordeal had become.

The chronicler wrote, "We passed all that day most anxiously. At night more people surrounded us than ever before, and we were no longer allowed to walk in the compound, within which we were, but confined within a small tiled court, with a multitude of people around us. We quite expected that on the following day we should be separated, or that some harm would befall us, for we noticed that our jailers were much annoyed with us. This, however, did not prevent our making a good supper off the things found in the village. Throughout that night we were guarded by over a hundred men, all armed with swords, two-edged battle axes, shields and bows and arrows. While some of these slept, others kept guard, each taking his turn of duty throughout the night."

One with a more positive outlook could perhaps convince themselves that the armed guards were there to protect da Gama and his companions. But as the situation seemed to be deteriorating, it is quite understandable why da Gama and his crew might have come to fear the worst. The next day, however, it seems that the misunderstandings were eased over, and it was made clear to da Gama that it was simply "the customs of the country" that certain protocols needed to be followed.

There was no mysterious plot afoot; the Indian Raja was just trying to make sure that his visitors followed typical procedure. The Raja was willing to make an exception, though, and agreed that if the Portuguese crew went ahead and brought their goods to the docks, the ships could remain at sea. Da Gama and his companions could be brought to them in the manner in which they requested. Upon returning to the craft waiting for their return, the chronicler captured the relief felt by all, writing, "At this we rejoiced greatly."

After a lack of interest was displayed in the landed goods, da Gama requested the Raja to send some of his men to deliver the trade goods to the city of Calicut, where other commerce was being conducted. This way, they would have a better chance of gaining the interest of passing merchants. The Raja graciously obliged this request.

The proceeds that the Portuguese gleaned were disappointing, but they did manage to raise enough money to buy some spices, gold-worked objects, and other valuable commodities. This small sampling of Indian goods would at least serve as proof of the potential wealth that could be gained by free and open trade with India.

At this point, da Gama was ready to leave, but he still had one more card he wished to play. He wanted to request for the Raja to allow him to leave behind some of his crew so that they could establish a permanent trading post. Da Gama sent a crew member by the name of Diogo Dias back ashore so that he could deliver this request to the Raja. Diogo was subsequently informed that to do such a thing, a "trading tax" would be required.

Diogo intended to return to the waiting ships to deliver this information to da Gama, but he ended up being held hostage in a nearby house. Diogo was apparently being held as an attempt to force the Portuguese to pay all of the fees that were due. Da Gama was quietly informed of what was happening, and he decided to play it off as if he was not in the least bit concerned. On August 15th, some of the Raja's entourage rowed up to da Gama's ships and offered to trade some goods. He had everyone pretend that everything was normal.

It is believed that these men were sent to da Gama in order to gauge the temperament of the visitors, and da Gama's cool composure managed to lull them into complacency. On August 19th, after twenty Indian traders and dignitaries boarded one of da Gama's ships, he suddenly turned on them and had his guests held hostage. Da Gama, of course, was operating on the cold calculus that he could use these hostages to get Diogo back. The gambit worked, and Diogo was successfully exchanged for some of the hostages that da Gama held.

But the key phrase here is "some of the hostages." Da Gama, proving just how ruthless he could be, made sure to keep a few on board as future bargaining chips and insisted that the rest of the hostages would be released after his remaining merchandise was restored to him. So, until all of his unsold goods were transported back to his ships, at the Raja's own expense at that, he was not going to release the rest of the hostages.

Da Gama was certainly playing hardball. For a guy who tried his best to impress the Raja upon his first meeting with him, da Gama's tactics had changed considerably. The actions that da Gama took next, however, are rather puzzling. Once the goods were rowed back up to the ships, Vasco da Gama suddenly decided to have his ships turn speed in the other direction, leaving the goods behind and keeping the terrified hostages on board.

This seems incredibly cruel and duplicitous on da Gama's part unless there was some other reason lost as to why he might have done this. Was the increasingly edgy and paranoid da Gama afraid he was about to fall into a trap? It remains a bit unclear. At any rate, this first seaborne voyage to India by Portugal achieved a major milestone, although it left much scandal and outrage in its wake.

Chapter 4 – Tragedy and Triumph

"And it all goes to pay the carriers, the ships and the dues of the sultan. So going the other way it's possible to strip out all these costs and middlemen. Which is why I hold the sultan; these kings and the Muslims will do all they can to rebuff the Portuguese king in this business. If the king continues it will be possible to sell spices at the port of Pisa many times more cheaply than at Cairo, because it's possible to get them there at a much lower cost."

-Girolamo Sernigi

Vasco da Gama and his crew returned to Portugal in the summer of 1499. This successful voyage was followed by yet another in 1500— this time led by a Portuguese nobleman, Pedro Álvares Cabral. This mission sought to fulfill the one objective that Vasco da Gama's mission had been unable to. Cabral and his associates would attempt to install a permanent Portuguese trading post.

The Portuguese had a good handle on how to circumnavigate the tip of Africa so that they could reach India by this time. It is interesting to note that the exact methodology was considered a state secret. The Portuguese knew how to make this treacherous voyage, but they did not want any other nation to know what they knew. All sailing charts and related information about how these expeditions were made were ordered to be kept secret under the pain of death.

For the Portuguese, their secret route to India was something akin to the Manhattan Project. And it was not entirely unlike the development of the nuclear bomb, for it, too, would come to change the world. Pedro Álvares Cabral did indeed follow the path laid out by Vasco da Gama, but the westward winds proved a little stronger than anticipated. His ships were actually pushed far enough west to reach the eastern coasts of Brazil.

This would prove to be a pivotal discovery, though, at the time, the crew had no idea where they had ended up. Here, the explorers would find a large amount of a form of red dyewood. The Portuguese already referred to this commodity as brazilwood or, as it was said in the Portuguese dialect of the time, *pau-brasil*. The whole territory came to be named after this red-hued brazilwood. But there was more to this land than redwood.

Brazil, of course, was already inhabited by various native groups. This Portuguese expedition would encounter some of them, and the crew was found to generally admire the society of the natives. Though the natives were far different from their own people, they were seen as a peaceful and even noble group of people. They were seen freely roaming the forests of Brazil without much worry or concern of anything.

As the expedition's chronicler, Pêro Vaz de Caminha, documented of the encounter, "They seem to me to be people of such innocence that, if we could understand them and they us, they would soon become Christians, because they do not seem to have or to understand any form of religion. For it is certain that this people is [sic] good and of pure simplicity, and there can easily be stamped upon them whatever belief we wish to give them."

Although Pêro no doubt thought he was being charitable at the time, his words today would be roundly condemned. While praising the locals for their "simplicity" and "innocence," he desired to "stamp upon them" the Portuguese belief systems. Of course, one must consider the context of the times in which these Portuguese explorers lived.

Christians in general and the Portuguese and Spanish in particular were locked in what they viewed as a life and death struggle with Islam. And as both Islam and Christianity continued to compete for dominance in this zero-sum game of religious outreach, these new unknown people with no apparent religious affiliation, such as those encountered by the Portuguese, were essentially seen as a group of religiously neutral individuals who needed to be coerced into the Christian fold.

At any rate, this accidental landing in Brazil would encourage another expedition in 1501 and yet another in 1503, leading to eventual settlements being established. But as it pertains to this particular voyage with Cabral at the helm, India was still the prime objective. And in early May, they left this strange new land to once again head southwest toward the southern tip of Africa.

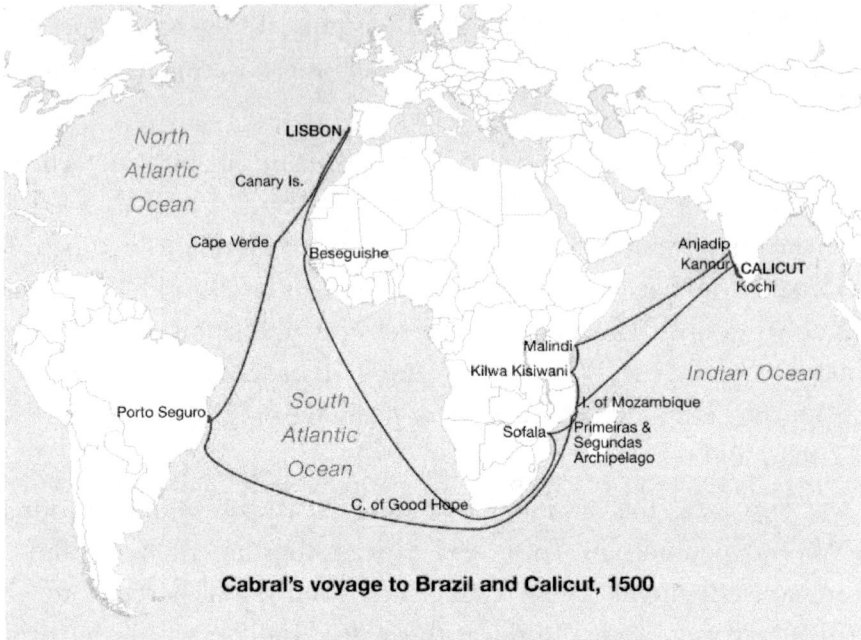

Cabral's route in 1500.

Several weeks later, they reached and then circumnavigated around the tip. By mid-June, the Portuguese had managed to make landfall on the other side in Mozambique. Here, the local sultan was hospitable enough, allowing them to replenish their stores of water and even giving them a local man to help lead them to the nearby trading port of Kilwa. After a brief pitstop in Kilwa, they then moved up the coast to the port of Malindi, where they obtained another local navigator to help ensure the smooth crossing of the Indian Ocean.

It seems that even though the Portuguese were doing their best to follow the instructions of their predecessors, they still depended upon some local help to make sure they stayed on track. Shortly after Cabral and his company arrived, they learned that the Indian Raja—the Samoothiri Raja—who had previously hosted Vasco da Gama had passed and that he had been replaced by his nephew.

One might think this was good news for Cabral and his crew since the relations between da Gama and the old Raja had become so antagonistic. But despite the new leadership, it was not long before tensions between Cabral and the new Raja began to become frayed as well. In the Portuguese proto-gunboat diplomacy style, Cabral met the new Raja with a more aggressive attitude. On behalf of the king of Portugal, Cabral demanded "preferential tax tariffs" as well as "low prices for spices," with the promise of a permanent Portuguese trading post to boot. But probably the most galling was Cabral's request to have the Muslim merchants banned from conducting trade since, as Pedro Cabral insisted, this "would comply with his duty as a Christian king."

The Portuguese, you see, were still locked into their misunderstanding that Hindus were some sort of strange Christian sect. They still believed that the Raja and his court were Christians. As such, they made demands of this supposed Christian Indian king, just as they would their Christian counterparts in Europe. By the time the Raja's interpreters translated half of the things that Cabral was saying, he was no doubt appalled. Who were these aggressive strangers? And who gave them the right to make such outrageous demands?

One could only imagine the Raja asking himself such questions. But the Raja realized that he was dealing with a foreign power that could bring considerable damage to his kingdom, so he settled upon a cautious form of appeasement, at least to buy himself some time. The Raja did not outright deny many of the demands, but he was not exactly clear on whether all of them would be granted. At any rate, after weeks of negotiations, Cabral's ships were loaded up with plenty of spices and other precious goods.

But there was a problem—the local Arab merchants, rightly realizing that the Portuguese were threatening to push them out of this lucrative trade, began to run interference and slow the loading of Cabral's ships. They also noticed that some of these same merchants had their own ships rapidly loaded up, stealthily sailing out of the harbor with a full load.

Cabral lodged an official complaint with the Raja about this, and the Raja, feeling the full pressure of his demanding guests, consented to allow the Portuguese to pursue any merchant craft seen to be engaging in this sort of unlawful behavior. It was not long before Cabral seized one of the crafts. This action, however, lit the fuse of long-simmering hostilities between the Portuguese and Arab merchants. Soon, a huge group of angry merchants stormed the recently established Portuguese trading post. They were hellbent upon taking their vengeance out on the hapless Portuguese stationed there.

The Portuguese traders were forced inside a nearby building, locking themselves behind a large gate. The Portuguese then clambered up onto the wall and began firing on the crowd with their crossbows, killing and injuring several. Cabral, in the meantime, received word about what was happening on the ground and sent some smaller boats equipped with swivel guns and had them fire into the crowd.

The guns could not effectively reach the rioters, so they did not deter them from continuing their siege of the compound. The attackers then set fire to the wall and actually managed to burn it to the ground. The wild crowd then charged up toward the building the Portuguese were now hiding in. It was at this point that the Portuguese inside decided to make a run for it, hoping to outrun their attackers and reach the gunboats that were nearby.

Running at full speed, they managed to get to the beach but were frustrated to find that the gunboats were still a distance away. They were forced to get into the water and swim for it. The mob managed to catch up to them at this point, and before they could swim toward safety, many were hacked to pieces with scimitars or even torn limb from limb with the bare hands of the angry rioters.

In the end, it has been estimated that some fifty Portuguese were killed in this massacre, while a mere twenty managed to make it to the safety of the boats. Cabral, of course, was quite infuriated, and he soon demanded the Raja to take action against these aggressors. But the Raja essentially kept quiet. It is likely he was unsure what to do, so he simply refused to respond. This led Cabral to seek vengeance on his own. He arbitrarily hunted down ten different craft belonging to the Arab merchants. He brought them to port and then had all on board the ship killed right then and there for all to see.

It was a truly dreadful scene. As one chronicler put it, "And thus we slew to the number of five hundred or six hundred men, and captured twenty or thirty who were hiding in the holds of the ships and also the merchandise; and thus we robbed the ships and took what they had within them. One had in it three elephants which we killed and ate, and we burned all nine of the unloaded ships."

The brutality of these actions would shock just about anyone. Even the elephants were not spared; they, too, were consumed, as well as the empty ships. It was overkill for a previous wrong that these particular men may not have had anything to do with.

As brutal as all of this is, one must keep in mind the background of Portugal and the Iberian Peninsula to understand their mindset at the time. The Portuguese truly felt that they were on the front lines of a holy war, and more often than not, they gave no quarter to their perceived enemies, either at home or abroad. Cabral, however, had a thirst for vengeance that seemed to go above and beyond even what was typical for the time. And after this particular display, he actually fired upon the city of Calicut itself, demolishing many buildings near the coast.

He then washed his hands of the Raja altogether and sailed north to the city of Cochin (Kochi), where the local potentate was a known rival of the Raja of Calicut. This was apparently planned all along; Cochin had been reserved as an alternative in case things did not work out in Calicut. Here at Cochin, the Portuguese would begin a classic divide and conquer strategy in regard to India. They would align themselves with one of the Raja's rivals so as to better insert themselves into India's geopolitical and global affairs.

Forgetting all about their failed attempt to install a trading post in Calicut, the Portuguese now put all of their focus on Cochin. And soon, friendly relations were established. The Portuguese were able to create a permanent trading post in Cochin, and they had their ships loaded up with precious goods without any delay. At Cochin, they were also first introduced to a few actual Indian Christians.

It was from this rare segment of Indian society that the Portuguese learned the truth. They discovered that while there was a very small population of Christians in India, they were an extreme minority. They soon began to understand more about the main religion of India—Hinduism—from these local Christians.

In the meantime, Cabral received a warning from the locals that the Raja of Calicut was planning to strike out against him and his crew. It was learned that a fleet of some eighty ships was on its way to launch an assault against them. Pedro Cabral did not want to stick around for an all-out naval battle, so he loaded his ships and quietly slipped away to avoid conflict.

Cabral made one more pitstop in nearby Cannanore (Kannur) to get some more goods before disembarking from India altogether. Cabral and company ended up returning to Portugal in the summer of 1501. It had been a hard journey, and of the thirteen ships that had left the previous year, only seven returned. The rest had been either lost or abandoned, with the survivors piling into the seven operable vessels to make their way back home.

Pedro Cabral's expedition was viewed as both a triumph and a tragedy. Many were aghast at the reports of what had happened to the Portuguese trading post in Calicut, but others still saw the potential for great wealth—including, of course, King Manuel of Portugal. The Portuguese were determined to press on. Cabral apparently had had enough, though. None other than Vasco da Gama would be tapped for the next major expedition to India.

Chapter 5 – Establishing Permanent Outposts

"My son is dead, as God willed and my sins deserve. The Venetians and the Sultan's Muslims killed him. As a result of this, the Muslims in these parts are hopeful of great help. It seems to me that this year we cannot avoid a trial of strength with them, which is the thing I most desire, because it seems to me that with God's help we have to remove them totally from the sea, so that they do not return to this land. And if our Lord is served by my ending my days in this way, I will have obtained the rest I seek."

-Francisco de Almeida

The already legendary Vasco da Gama disembarked for his second grand expedition to India in early 1502. As usual, the crew sailed around North Africa, swung west at the equator, then used the westerly winds to launch themselves southeast toward the tip of South Africa. After rounding the cape, Vasco da Gama went to the now familiar stomping grounds of Mozambique and took some time to reestablish relations with the local leaders.

From here, he went on to the port of Kilwa, where he sought the audience of the local sultan. Vasco da Gama was able to intimidate the sultan enough to convince him to cooperate, and a lasting trade relationship was established. The Portuguese ships then sailed up to the port of Malindi, where they were given a more or less friendly welcome. By September, they had reached Mt. Deli, where they rested for a bit and restocked their dwindling supplies.

In the vicinity of Mt. Deli, the crew spotted a large Arab ship sailing nearby. The ship was called the *Miri*, and it was full of religious pilgrims who were traversing across the Indian Ocean from Calicut. They were on their way to Mecca. Da Gama, displaying his full ruthlessness and utter contempt for Muslims, ordered his ships to attack this unarmed vessel.

After looting the now disabled ship, Vasco da Gama ordered it to be set ablaze and proceeded to watch as everyone on board suffered a terrible death. Many brutal incidents often occurred between Muslims and Christians in those days, but this incident was viewed to be outrageous, even in that day and age. Many among Vasco da Gama's own crew began to wonder just how cruel and cold-hearted their captain really was. One remarked over the senseless violence that some of the wealthier crew probably would have been more than willing to pay a big ransom if the ship were spared. The chronicler thought it was big enough "to ransom all of the Christians held in Fez."

The writer was referring to Fez, Morocco, where many kidnapped Christians had been taken by Muslim forces and held for ransom. As cruel as kidnapping someone for profit might be, at least there was some hope that the victims might be returned to their family members. Vasco da Gama was taking things much further by refusing to even consider a ransom. He was engaging in a shade of brutality that was darker than usual.

The sad fate of the *Miri* was sealed on October 3ʳᵈ when it was set ablaze and turned into nothing more than flaming ash and cinders floating on the waters. Vasco da Gama's own chronicler lamented the monstrous callousness displayed, acknowledging, "That with great cruelty and without any pity the admiral burned the ship and all who were in it." After this outright atrocity was committed, Vasco da Gama crossed the Indian Ocean and landed in the Port of Cannanore to restock. He was soon on his way to Calicut.

It seems that Vasco da Gama was eager to get vengeance for past slights, as he really laid down the hammer on the Raja once he reached Calicut. By now, the residents of Calicut had received word of what had happened to the *Miri* and were practically frightened into submission. The Raja sent a letter to da Gama in which he declared his desire for peaceful relations. In his overtures, he even offered to reimburse da Gama for the goods that had been abandoned on his previous expedition.

As for the lives that were lost on both sides, the Raja was more realistic in his acknowledgment that this could not be rightfully reimbursed. But the Raja was magnanimous enough to offer an olive branch and suggest that they should both essentially forgive and forget. Even though the Raja was not actually the Christian king that da Gama had once taken him for, these were most certainly Christian values on display. After all, the greatest attribute of Christianity is forgiveness.

But Vasco da Gama ultimately proved how unchristian he could be, as he let his bitter and vengeful nature get the better of him. And his mind for vengeance was ultimately made up when his Indian ally in Cochin sent word to Vasco da Gama that the Raja of Calicut had sent a secret letter to him around the same time, suggesting that the rivals forget their differences and join forces against the Portuguese. Having heard about this, Vasco da Gama was not in any mood for mercy.

Messengers from the Raja appeared at the port to record Vasco da Gama's demands. They found that these demands were not going to be easy ones. Vasco da Gama demanded something to which the Raja could never agree. He not only demanded financial compensation for the attack on the previous Portuguese outpost, but he also demanded that all Muslim merchants be barred from further trade. In the draconian statement he handed off to the Raja's emissaries, Vasco da

Gama declared that "otherwise he did not wish to make peace or any agreement with him, because Muslims were enemies of Christians and vice versa since the world began."

The Raja obviously could not take such absurd and belligerent demands seriously. But at the same time, he did not have any more bargaining chips left against the gunboat diplomacy of the Portuguese. He sent back an apologetic response, but he insisted that he could not expel the Muslim merchants. Upon receiving this refusal to his unreasonable demands, Vasco da Gama promptly seized the dignitaries of the Raja and set in motion his own personal war against the Indian potentate.

He had the ship's guns lowered and began blasting everything in reach into smithereens. There was eventually a lull in the fighting, and the Raja sent word that there would be a peaceful resolution. But the Raja, desperate to get rid of the Portuguese, had something else in mind. In the dead of night, he had a squadron of some eighty ships sneak up on the Portuguese craft.

The ships opened fire at close range and threatened to sink the Portuguese ships. The only thing that saved the surrounded Portuguese craft was the sudden arrival of ships under the command of Vicente Sodré, who had stayed behind in Cannanore. Vicente arrived just in time to engage the Raja's craft, allowing Vasco da Gama's ships to break free and then turn around and attack the Raja's ships. The Raja's ships were no match and were forced to flee.

The infuriated Vasco da Gama fired off another message for the Raja in the meantime, stating, "Oh miserable man, you had me called and I came at your request. You have done all that you could, and you would have done more if you could. You have had the punishment that you deserve: when I return here I will pay your due—and it won't be in money." Da Gama ultimately left India behind in the spring of 1503; behind him, he left a trading post in Cochin and Cannanore, while Calicut was practically buried in rubble.

After da Gama's departure, the fragile Portuguese outpost at the allied Indian port of Cochin was vulnerable to reprisal. And soon after, the Raja struck, launching a massive assault on Cochin. The Portuguese and their Indian allies were forced to flee to the island of Vypin that summer, where they remained under constant siege. In September of 1503, their lives were secured when Francisco de Albuquerque, along with two other ships, arrived fresh from Portugal.

These ships were then followed by four other Portuguese ships, which were led by Francisco's cousin, Afonso de Albuquerque. This relief force allowed the beleaguered defenders to return to Cochin, but the extra manpower would not be able to stay. By the spring of 1504, the ships once again loaded up with spices and readied themselves to head back to Portugal.

It is a bit mind-boggling that after such ferocious attacks, the Portuguese were still doing business with the Raja of Calicut, but this was precisely the case. Even after all of this fighting, the Raja and the Portuguese craft had entered into what historian and writer Roger Crowley has referred to as a "cynical truce." It was quite cynical on the part of the Portuguese traders since the Portuguese knew that as soon as they got their spices and left, the Raja would wage war on their Portuguese countrymen who remained at Cochin. And it was cynical on the part of the Raja as well since he was trading goods with men whose countrymen he was still plotting to slaughter.

But this was indeed the state of affairs at the time. And sure enough, as soon as spring arrived, the Portuguese ships laden with spices left for Lisbon, Portugal, once again. Around one hundred Portuguese were left to defend Cochin, along with a few small craft. All of them were directed by Duarte Pacheo Pereira. It has been said that the cynical Portuguese who sailed their ships back to Portugal were almost certain that the men left behind would all be dead by the time they returned.

But the cunning and strategic Duarte Pacheo Pereira would prove them wrong. The Raja did indeed launch his forces against Cochin shortly after the spice ships left, striking out against the absurdly small garrison on Cochin that March. Considering the fact that the Raja was sending tens of thousands of troops against a pitiful band of Portuguese defenders, the Indian ruler of Cochin actually recommended that they all abandon the post and leave him to beg the Raja for forgiveness.

This was ostensibly an act of mercy on this potentate's part since he figured that the Portuguese would meet certain death—or perhaps even worse—should they stay to face the Raja of Calicut's wrath. However, Duarte was not one to back down, and he pledged his allegiance to the leader of Cochin, declaring, "We will die serving you if necessary." Duarte worked like a madman and began to set about erecting defenses all over Cochin, placing makeshift stockades of stakes wrapped in steel chains at every strategic point. He then positioned all of the artillery in narrow fords and waited for the enemy forces to arrive.

The Raja of Calicut's army was massive. But other than just marching headlong toward Cochin, their strategy was lacking. And despite their best attempts to rush through the defenses Duarte had laid, they were consistently mowed down by heavy Portuguese artillery at every turn.

Incredibly enough, this small group of Portuguese defenders managed to successfully repulse the Raja's troops on seven different occasions. By July of 1504, the humiliated Raja had had enough, and he called off the attack. He was so thoroughly disgraced that he actually resigned from office, handed power over to his nephew, and became a Hindu monk.

Shortly after the Raja's defeat, a relief force from Portugal arrived with huge ships and massive artillery bristling from their decks. These reinforcements probably expected to find Duarte and the rest of the defenders dead, but they instead found them victorious.

The Portuguese now had a frightening mystique of being unstoppable, and many more local Indian rulers began to openly embrace the Portuguese out of fear for their cities and people. In the meantime, the Muslim merchants from Mecca were being systematically shut out, and many were forced to leave their old outposts behind, as the ban on Muslim merchants that Vasco da Gama had called for essentially came into being.

Several more Portuguese settlements in India were established. These settlements were put under the administration of Francisco de Almeida, the first viceroy or governor of what would become Portuguese India. King Manuel of Portugal himself delegated this authority, fully knowing that due to the distance and impossibility of back-and-forth communication, a permanent Portuguese presence with local Portuguese leadership must be established.

Almeida left for the Indian outposts in March of 1505. Before landing in India, however, he had some business to take care of on the East African coast. Almeida visited the port of Kilwa. Vasco da Gama had established relations with Kilwa in previous years, and the sultan there had promised trade as well as an annual tribute to the Portuguese. This sultan had since put an end to these friendly relations.

Almeida sought to pick up where Vasco da Gama had left off, landing his ships in full force and demanding tribute. The situation quickly broke down from here, and Almeida ended up attacking the port. Almeida himself led the charge, and he personally planted a Portuguese flag on Kilwa soil. The sultan and many of the residents fled before them, allowing the Portuguese to seize the deserted settlement.

The Portuguese hastily constructed a fort and made loyal subjects of those who remained. They also installed a local merchant as their new point man in Kilwa. Almeida himself was ecstatic over these results. This can be seen in the letter he fired off to the king of Portugal shortly after, stating, "Sire, Kilwa has the best port of any place I know of in the world, and the fairest land."

From here, Almeida approached the port of Mombasa. Here, however, he met fierce resistance from the local sultan, who tried to throw everything he could at Almeida. The Portuguese were once again able to use their shipboard cannons, as well as muskets on the ground, to blast the inhabitants into submission. On the heels of this seizure, Almeida and company would cross the Indian Ocean and then make landfall in India proper later that summer. It could be said that this was the moment that the Portuguese overseas empire began in earnest.

Chapter 6 – Conflicts of Interest

"I am a man who, if you entrusted me with a dozen kingdoms, would know how to govern them with great prudence, discretion and knowledge. This is not because of any special merits of my own but because I am very experienced in such matters and of an age to tell good from bad."

-Afonso de Albuquerque

Francisco de Almeida left his post as governor in 1509, and he was replaced by Afonso de Albuquerque. Just prior to leaving his post, Almeida struck a stunning blow to the local Islamic powers by using his naval forces to sink a joint Egyptian/Gujrati (Indian) fleet in February of 1509. This fleet was essentially the only real naval opposition left in the region that could have stood up against the powerful Portuguese galleons.

Only one of the Gujarati carracks proved to be formidable. This was a twin-decked behemoth that held some four hundred fighting men. The ship was said to have held out against the Portuguese until the very end of the battle. The ship itself was too close to shore for the Portuguese to safely board and attempt to take over. In the end, they were forced to simply continue taking potshots at the craft from a distance.

It took a whole lot of effort, but the ship finally began to sink. It never capsized; it just slowly began its descent under the waves. This allowed those on board to escape the doomed ship by simply hopping off and swimming to shore. These were the lucky ones, as it is estimated that some 1,300 Gujaratis perished during the course of the fighting. And as for the Portuguese? It is estimated that around one hundred Portuguese lost their lives, with maybe around three hundred being severely injured. This was indeed a clear and indisputable victory for the Portuguese fleet.

On the heels of this victory, Almeida's term as governor ended, and it was time for his successor, Albuquerque, to succeed him. However, Almeida was not quite ready to hand over power, and he bluntly informed the would-be governor that he would have to wait to assume office until the weather was favorable enough for him to set sail back to Lisbon.

This meant that Almeida would remain the acting governor until the end of the monsoon season. This dicey situation of having two governors in the Portuguese Indies would not be resolved until November of that year when a man by the name of Fernandes Coutinho, the so-called Marshal of Portugal, arrived on the scene. Fernandes had been given full royal authority to ensure that the peaceful transition between Almeida and Albuquerque took place.

The day after Albuquerque took official control as governor, Almeida hopped onto a ship and sailed away from India. Interestingly enough, it has been said that a fortune teller of some sort had actually warned Almeida against the trip, predicting that he would perish before reaching Portugal. It is a bit odd that such supposedly fervent Christians would resort to fortune tellers, but in the long lonely nights at their posts, it seems that such things often became hard to resist.

At any rate, the prediction was seemingly fulfilled, and Almeida would indeed perish on the trip. The incident occurred in March of 1510, shortly after rounding Africa's Cape of Good Hope. The crew landed to gather wood, water, and other resources when they were ambushed by some locals. They were taken by complete surprise, and in the vicious attack, it is said that some fifty crew members—including Almeida—were killed.

It is rather ironic that so many men died doing such a simple task. During the massive naval battle in which Almeida put down the Egyptian/Gujarati fleet, around one hundred Portuguese perished, but that was facing large ships and cannons. Here, about half that number were killed just getting a drink of water. At any rate, Almeida would not see Portugal again; he was buried not far from where he was slain on the African coast.

Although Albuquerque was in charge as governor, the marshal brought instructions directly from the king of Portugal that Albuquerque was supposed to follow. It had been determined that Calicut should be seized. The Raja of Calicut had long resisted the Portuguese, but now these newcomers to the Indies were determined to quite literally force the doors of Calicut wide open.

The plan was to land a joint armada, with part of the fleet led by Albuquerque and the other part led by Marshal Coutinho. Upon landing, both groups were to storm Calicut together, taking the fight all the way to the Cerame—the Raja's own personal pavilion where he held audiences. It is incredible to think of how rapidly the situation had changed since Vasco da Gama first met with the Raja on bended knee in humble humility.

The Portuguese were confident in their force of arms. It seems they were done with any and all efforts of diplomacy and were ready to storm the pavilion outright. On January 2nd, 1510, under cover of darkness, Albuquerque's squadron made landfall off the shores of Calicut just south of the Cerame. Marshal Coutinho was then supposed to land his contingent to the north of the Cerame so that it would be attacked from both sides at the same time.

Such a feat would have no doubt been absolutely devastating, but Governor Albuquerque's men had other plans. These rough and tumble warriors were just itching for a fight, and despite their rules to stand down and wait for the Coutinho's forces to arrive, they began to make inroads toward the pavilion of their own accord. Coutinho was delayed, though, because his ship accidentally overshot its landing, ending up too far north.

In the meantime, Albuquerque was beginning to lose control of his rowdy troops, who were more than ready to sack Calicut. Realizing that any attempt to stop them might backfire with an all-out mutiny, he decided to go ahead and order them to attack. The energized Portuguese assailants then rushed forward with pikes, swords, and firearms, ready to mow down anyone that stood in their way.

The Raja had placed several barricades and heavily armed guards in the path of the Portuguese, but they proved ineffective at holding their ground against this tidal wave of aggression. Many were killed in the attempt. While Coutinho's troops were still floundering in the waters, Albuquerque's men reached the pavilion and actually ripped the ornate doors from their hinges with their axes. These were then hurriedly sent back to the ships, both as loot and as a souvenir of their conquest.

Albuquerque did not want his troops to proceed any farther without the reinforcements of Coutinho, and he put a contingent of troops at the gates to keep them from moving forward. Marshal Coutinho, in the meantime, had finally arrived, but by now, he could hear the sounds of a battle already underway. Coutinho became infuriated, thinking that Albuquerque was attempting to somehow outdo him.

Albuquerque anticipated as much, and he had a message sent to Coutinho that sought to give him credit for the events, stating, "You are the first captain to have landed men and entered the city of Calicut, and you have gained what you sought—the doors of the Cerame are now on board." But this attempt to share credit with Marshal Coutinho only infuriated him further. Taking it as an insult, Coutinho is said to have muttered in disgust, "What is this Afonso de Albuquerque? Your words are nothing but a puff of air."

At any rate, Albuquerque did not have the intended effect of making the late-coming marshal feel as if he were part of the team. Instead, Coutinho shot back, "This honor is yours. I don't want any of it." The fact that such a petty grievance would jeopardize the mission seems absolutely absurd, but for these men, who lived and breathed their own unique sense of honor when it came to warfare, such matters were indeed important. And the fact that Marshal Coutinho was left out during the initial siege rendered him absolutely uncooperative with Albuquerque. He had other plans.

In a bid to gain glory for himself and his contingent, he ordered the four hundred men under his command to march all the way to the Raja's palace, which was situated some three miles farther inland. This was a dangerous proposition since it meant the troops would have to pour through the narrow streets and alleys of Calicut to get there. Put in such a position, they could be ambushed rather easily. The rapid march of Coutinho was fairly successful, and despite some loss of life, he was indeed able to get to the courtyard of the palace with most of his troops intact.

It was here, however, that all hell broke loose, as the Raja's royal guard surged out to greet them. They set off a blistering barrage of arrows, and many of the Portuguese fighters soon took on the appearance of porcupines with shafts sticking out of their armor and, for the less fortunate, out of their bare flesh. The Portuguese were finally able to push the defenders back, forcing the guards to turn their attention to evacuating the Raja rather than defending the palace.

With its defenders gone, the Portuguese burst into the palace and, in a complete frenzy, began grabbing up all of the treasure that they could find. The Raja, who had been safely evacuated from the premises, began to redirect his royal guard. He sent a large force of them (about four hundred in total) back to the palace to take on the distracted Portuguese, who were busy sifting through the palace treasures. Ironically enough, the besiegers would soon be under siege themselves.

Coutinho's luck had not completely run out yet, as Albuquerque and a contingent of his own troops had just arrived on the scene. Albuquerque realized how dire the situation was, and he quickly set up a perimeter. He and his men were able to temporarily hold the Raja's forces back. Albuquerque knew that this perimeter would not last long, so he sent word to Coutinho that his time was up and that they all needed to evacuate Calicut immediately.

Since he was still looting the palace, Marshal Coutinho refused to heed the warning. This led an entirely frustrated and flabbergasted Albuquerque to head into the palace himself and directly order the marshal to make a tactical withdrawal. Albuquerque pleaded with Coutinho, saying, "In the name of the king, we ask you to leave. We mustn't stay here a moment longer. If we don't, we're all dead. The route by which you came is all on fire, and we're going to have great trouble getting away."

To these desperate words, Coutinho is said to have laughed. In full bravado, he declared that he would make sure that he was the "last to leave" and that after looting all the treasures from the palace, he would set the whole place ablaze. Bewildered, Albuquerque ordered his men to begin the evacuation, leading in the front, with the marshal's men following from behind. True to his word, Marshal Coutinho remained in the rear, flanked by just a small contingent of troops.

Some of these Portuguese fighters wielded a heavy piece of artillery called a *berço*, which proved quite effective in knocking back the surge of attackers that swarmed on all sides as the Portuguese passed through the narrow streets and alleys of Calicut. However, as the winding path narrowed, the heavy artillery did not have enough room for the men to operate them, and they had to be left behind. Without this firepower to back them up, the Raja's forces were able to swoop down on them with increasing aggression.

At one point, a group of them managed to outflank Marshal Coutinho and his entourage. Marshal Coutinho is said to have swung around to face his attacker, only to have the back of his foot chopped right off by one of the many sword-wielding hands that thrust at him. This caused the marshal, who was a large, heavy man, to fall right to the ground. His defenders tried to help their fallen leader, but the big man proved to be too difficult to pick up.

Nevertheless, his guards felt compelled to stand and fight around their injured liege. They fought until they, too, were cut down. Soon, all of these slain Portuguese would have their decapitated heads hauled off by their jubilant opponents. Albuquerque, who was at the front of the retreating Portuguese column, soon learned of what was happening and attempted to lead troops to the rear to see if they could be of assistance.

They could not make much headway, and Albuquerque himself was soon subject to a grievous injury. An arrow sank through his left arm, and a dart hit him in the neck. Just as he was coming to grips with these injuries, a bullet managed to strike him right in the chest. As Albuquerque fell to the ground, it was believed that the governor was dead. The sight of the slain commander caused the Raja's troops to be energized.

They surged forward in a frenzy to seek more vengeance against their enemies. Before they could seize the fallen Albuquerque, four of his loyal guards put him up on a large shield. They ran through the whirlwind of arrows, darts, and bullets, rushing Governor Albuquerque toward the ships waiting on the coast. The closer they got to the beach, the safer they were. The longboats were situated with *berço* artillery, which were ready to provide cover for the retreating Portuguese.

Soon, the large cannons from the waiting galleys began to erupt, annihilating any of the pursuing Indian warriors who dared to get too close. Upon returning to the safety of the waiting ships, in what was perceived to be a miracle to all involved, it was discovered that Albuquerque was not mortally wounded after all. Governor

Albuquerque would, in fact, recover. His left arm would never be the same, but he would go on to live and rule Portuguese India.

Chapter 7 – Making Major Inroads

"It seems to me that if you make yourself powerful in the Red Sea, you will have all the riches of the world in your hands, because all the gold of Prester John will be available to you—such a huge sum that I don't dare speak of it—traded for spices and the merchandise of India. I take the liberty of writing like this to you your Highness, because I have seen India on both sides of the Ganges and I observe how our Lord is helping you and placing it in your grasp. Great tranquility and stability have come over India since your Highness gained Goa and Malacca and ordered us to ender the Red Sea, seek out the Sultan's fleet and cut the shipping lanes to Jeddah and Mecca. It is no small service that you will perform for our Lord in destroying the seat of perdition and all their depravity."

-Afonso de Albuquerque

India's most powerful self-ruling polity at the time of Portuguese imperial expansion under Governor Afonso de Albuquerque was that of the Hindu-based Vijayanagara Empire. As mighty as this polity was, it was landlocked at the time, and it was mostly concentrated on the eastern side of India. A rival of Vijayanagara, the Bijapur Sultanate, which was situated just to the west of Vijayanagara, had a powerful seaport on the southwestern side of India called Goa. This city was situated between the settlements of Kerala and Gujarat.

Goa was indeed a strategic outpost, and the fact that it sat on an island in the middle of two formidable rivers made it a fortress that could be easily defended. If the Portuguese had such a piece of real estate under their control, they would be much better positioned to get a handle on the Indian spice trade. The Portuguese established friendly relations with Vijayanagara, and it was not long before they began to plot with their new ally for the seizure of Goa.

Goa itself had been fought over between the Vijayanagara Empire and the Bijapur Sultanate many times. It just so happened to be under the control of the Bijapur Sultanate when the Portuguese began plotting to take it. Governor Albuquerque would end up waging open warfare against the Bijapur Sultanate, and he would manage to successfully seize the port from its grasp.

Besides aligning himself with the Hindu rulers of the Vijayanagara Empire, Governor Albuquerque had a surprising ally in the form of an Indian pirate by the name of Timoji. Timoji provided his own band of two thousand fighters, who attacked Goa on the ground while Portuguese ships blasted the Bijapur defenders from the waters. It was not long before Goa's defense gave out completely, and those who remained sued for peace.

Albuquerque, unlike previous Portuguese belligerents, demonstrated a much more tolerant approach. He declared that under Portuguese rule, the residents of Goa had nothing to fear and that he would make sure that both the Hindu faith as well as the Muslim faith would be tolerated. For a group of religious zealots whose own king had commissioned them to wage a holy war against Islam in the Indian Ocean, this was a great departure from what had been the typical stance of the Portuguese against other religions in general and most certainly Islam in particular.

Along with these peaceful overtures toward the faithful, Albuquerque also pledged to help out the residents of Goa by lowering the amount of taxes levied against them. Governor Albuquerque officially took up residence as the ruler of Goa on March 1ˢᵗ, 1510.

Many of the Hindu-believing Indians were relieved to be rid of the growing Islamic incursion that had been in their midst. Although Albuquerque was working for the Catholic Portuguese king and, by extension, the pope, he quickly found it more expedient for his more temporal purposes to practice a form of religious tolerance when it came to Hindu beliefs.

However, Albuquerque's religious tolerance proved to have its limits when it came to the practice of immolation, which was sometimes carried out by Hindu widows. This involved a widow throwing herself on her husband's funeral pyre and being burned alive. Albuquerque, just like the British centuries later, made sure that this lethal ceremony was shut down.

To further endear himself to the people, Albuquerque eased taxation and created his own currency. The currency, in full recognition of the crusading spirit that drove the Portuguese, was called the *cruzado*. Interestingly enough, Albuquerque launched a festive parade of sorts to introduce the coin to the populace. He had men carry the new form of currency in silver basins, while a full band, along with circus-style performers, followed the procession. Heralds declared in both Portuguese and the local tongue that the coins were "the new currency of the king our lord, who ordered that it should run in Goa and its territories."

Governor Albuquerque's mention of "the king our lord" was, of course, his effort of giving faraway King Manuel of Portugal credit for the seizure of Goa. Governor Albuquerque would come to rule Goa as if he were the king himself, though.

In the meantime, the man that Albuquerque had deposed—Yusuf Adil Shah—was already planning his return. And by April 1510, he had assembled a large force, with freshly recruited troops from Persia and remote regions of Central Asia. Incredibly enough, the force he cobbled together was said to be forty thousand strong. To say that this massive recruitment was slightly overkill on Adil Shah's part is an understatement, but he obviously did not intend to lose—the huge army he brought bore testament to this. This army was led by Adil Shah's loyal general, Palud Khan. This massive army, which came on a huge armada, first cut through the Hindu pirate Timoji's fleet as if it were nothing.

The force then managed to reach the outskirts of Goa proper. General Khan showed some surprising restrain, offering Governor Albuquerque the opportunity to not only retreat but also save considerable face. Khan knew that his forces would not be able to lose, but he most likely figured that he could probably take Goa without having to fire a shot if he could just convince the Portuguese that they were beaten.

General Khan even sweetened the deal by offering to find the Portuguese somewhere else farther down the coast where they could build a fortress. Now, it is unclear whether the general would actually make good on this deal; he very well could have changed his mind later and simply blow the Portuguese out of the water upon their retreat. Governor Albuquerque, for one, was not about to put his trust in General Khan's offer.

So, despite the incredible odds against them, Albuquerque obstinately refused to come to terms with his opponents. It has been said that General Khan was amazed at the audacity and boldness the Portuguese displayed in the face of certain defeat, but nevertheless, he ordered his troops forward so that the invasion of Goa could commence. In early May, with the monsoon rains pouring from the skies, the massive horde attacked Goa.

The pitiful group of defenders situated on the outer perimeter of the outpost was quickly overrun and decimated. It was not long before what remained of the Portuguese fighters found themselves seeking refuge in Goa's citadel. They held their ground here for several days, but they eventually came to terms with the fact that the walls around them were about to come crumbling down. Governor Albuquerque finally accepted reality and organized a plan to evacuate Goa.

The Portuguese fought a desperate rear-guard action all the way, but the Portuguese fleet was able to successfully sail to safer harbors on May 31st. Prior to leaving, some of Albuquerque's subordinates had actually suggested firing on Goa, but Albuquerque stayed their hand, insisting that they did not want to destroy structures that they would soon be coming back to reclaim.

Yes, Albuquerque, even while in full retreat, was determined to take back Goa at all costs. After deserting Goa, Albuquerque ended up docking at the island of Anjediva. Shortly after their arrival, they were met by a small fleet of Portuguese ships captained by Diogo Mendes de Vasconcelos. Diogo and company had just returned from even farther east, specifically from Malacca, a trading hub situated on the Malay Peninsula.

Diogo had been on a separate mission authorized by the king of Portugal to set up shop in Malacca, but he had been driven out. Hearing of this defeat while also still reflecting on his own expulsion from Goa, Albuquerque was immediately interested in backing a second attempt on Malacca. But before such a thing could be carried out, the governor's main focus was retaking Goa.

After Albuquerque's trusted informant Timoji brought him word that hostilities had erupted between Adil Shah and the Vijayanagara Empire, he knew that the moment to reclaim Goa was already at hand. Even so, it took a couple more months for Albuquerque to get his forces prepared for this latest attempt at seizing Goa. Back at his temporary headquarters in Cochin, Albuquerque assembled a war council on October 10th, where he cobbled together a group of captains loyal to him who were willing to take part in the fight. The governor then fired off a letter to King Manuel back in Lisbon to document his reasoning.

This missive read, in part, "You will see how good it is, your highness, that if you are lord of Goa, you throw the whole realm of

India into confusion. There is nowhere on the coasts as good or secure as Goa, because it's an island. If you lost the whole of India, you could reconquer it from there."

Soon after setting down his rationale, Albuquerque led his forces back to Goa, approaching this fortified island on November 24th, 1510. The Portuguese fleet, along with auxiliary forces of local allies, then launched a two-pronged attack on Goa on November 25th. Adil Shah had directed his men to erect defensive barricades, but once the Portuguese made landfall, the rapid rush of energized Portuguese fighters was able to easily knock them down.

They surged onward to the city gates of Goa. Here, one daring Portuguese fighter seemed to use his javelin as a long jumper would in the Olympics. He thrust the javelin into the city walls and actually managed to propel himself up into the air over it. This daring soul then clambered up onto a parapet, and with a Portuguese flag in hand, he began shouting, "Portugal! Portugal! Victory!"

It has been said that the city defenders were so stunned that many of them turned away from their posts defending the gates to gape at this crazed Portuguese fighter suddenly towering above them, right within the city walls. It was in this moment of distraction that the Portuguese tore through the city gates and surged into Goa. The fighting that ensued was bitter, bloody, and close quarters.

The defenders fought vigorously, but soon the ferocious onslaught had them on their heels. They sought to retreat across the waterways. Once they reached dry land, many were cut down by local Portuguese allies who met them on the other side. It took several hours, but Albuquerque successfully retook Goa and decisively defeated his enemy.

It was not long after Goa was back in the Portuguese fold that Albuquerque began to once again discuss the prospect of taking Malacca with Diogo Mendes de Vasconcelos. There were already sixty Portuguese hostages being held by the sultan of Malacca, Mahmud, from the previous failed attempt. Albuquerque sailed off to

Malaysia in April of 1511 to repatriate his countrymen and make Malacca his own. With him were eighteen ships filled with some seven hundred Portuguese soldiers, along with three hundred auxiliary fighters picked up from the Malabar coast.

Here, they were met with a new fighting element: the high-walled, huge junks (a type of ship) of East Asia. These ships proved much more resistant to artillery. As one of the Portuguese put it at the time, they were "no less strong than a castle, because it is of three or four decks one on top of another so that artillery does not harm it." At any rate, the fleet successfully made their way to Malacca on July 1ˢᵗ, and the mission to seize this valuable outpost commenced shortly thereafter.

However, the group briefly paused their advance after the sultan reached out for a peaceful solution. The sultan was no doubt intimidated by the huge fleet, and he now sought to use his Portuguese prisoners from the previous failed expedition as a bargaining chip. Sultan Mahmud wanted to cut a deal with the Portuguese in which the safe passage of ships would be allowed in exchange for the peaceful repatriation of the Portuguese prisoners of war.

Albuquerque insisted that the Portuguese prisoners must be given to him safe and sound before he entered into any further agreements. The sultan was not about to agree to such terms, yet he delayed and dragged on the discussions as much as possible in the hopes that the bad monsoon weather would arrive, thereby forcing the Portuguese to call the whole thing off. Albuquerque was well aware of this delaying tactic, and after a couple of weeks of stalled negotiations, he decided to commence with the bombardment of the city.

Once Sultan Mahmud's city was wrecked, he began to sing a different tune. He actually dressed up the prisoners of war in fine clothes and sent them off to Albuquerque. However, just as the sultan must have feared, this was not enough for Albuquerque. Now, Albuquerque was demanding that the sultan not only establish a

Portuguese trading post but also sponsor the building of a Portuguese fortress, as well as give them money to cover all of the damages that they had suffered.

The bitter irony was not lost on Sultan Mahmud since it was obviously the Portuguese who had caused most of the damage. These were obviously terms that the sultan could not accept. As such, he immediately began fortifying Malacca with trenches and defensive barriers. He also laid out elaborate traps for the Portuguese on the shores by installing iron spikes covered in hay and other rubbish, as well as sacks of gunpowder to work as makeshift landmines.

The strategic thrust in the seizure of Malacca was the taking of the grand bridge that ran toward the center of the settlement. This bridge crossed over the river that divided the city. It was realized that by taking this bridge, the Portuguese would essentially divide Malacca in half. It was in pursuit of this purpose that Albuquerque split his troops into two groups. One would make landfall on the western side of the river, while the other would make landfall on the right.

Upon hitting the beaches, the Portuguese and their allies were bombarded with cannon blasts, arrows, and poisonous darts shot from blowguns when they got too close. The cannons were largely inefficient in causing much damage. The Portuguese were used to facing off against arrows; during most battles in this period, arrows were the main offensive weapon of their opponents.

However, the poisonous darts caused great fear among the Portuguese. The weapons could only be used in fairly close range, but they were quick and stealthy. The dart itself did not inflict much pain, but those injected with its venom would soon start feeling the effects. And as their condition worsened, most would drop dead in a matter of days. This slow, painful, and seemingly irreversible death sentence terrified these hardened fighters the most.

Nevertheless, they pushed on. Upon reaching the bridge, the most fantastic battle scene took shape when the Portuguese forces were confronted by Sultan Mahmud's war elephants. These huge elephants had been outfitted to serve as living tanks and literally ran over anyone who approached. Many of the Portuguese fighters fled before these awesome beasts, but a few of them were bold. Instead of fleeing, they took their long lance and shoved it right into the lead elephant's eyes and stomach.

This caused the animal to become enraged and bewildered from the terrible blows it had sustained. It then turned on its own rider, knocking him off. Without the rider, the elephant became uncontrollable. Like a contagion, the madness spread. Soon the defenders were in a full-on panic, running from their own elephants. The Portuguese took control of the bridge soon after.

But even though the Portuguese had their opponents on the run, it was the very elements of Malacca that were taking a heavy toll. By this point, it was the middle of the day, and the sun was bearing down on the fighters. Already worn out from their fighting and standing there on that bridge with their previous adrenaline draining away, the awful heat began to sink into their systems. Feeling like they were being baked alive in their armor, the Portuguese realized that they were unable to progress any further.

Albuquerque realized this much as well, and as much as it grieved him to do so, he was forced to call off the attack. As the Portuguese withdrew, the sultan was able to rebuild his defenses once again while he awaited the next round of the siege. That next round came on August 10th, 1511. This time, the Portuguese were able to break through Sultan Mahmud's barricades and charge right into the city. After several hard-fought battles at close range, Malacca was in Portuguese hands.

The Portuguese were greatly assisted by local Hindu merchants in the establishment of this outpost. They helped the Portuguese become the new middlemen in regional trade goods. While they consolidated their position in the region, the Portuguese constructed a sturdy fortress, which they named the A Famosa.

In good time, Malacca would be used as a springboard to explore nearby Indonesia, especially the Maluku Islands (Moluccas). They had to put down local resistance first, though, which was done in stunning fashion in January of 1513 when Portuguese ships managed to wipe out an entire fleet of Javanese ships. That same year, on the other side of the Indian Ocean, a Portuguese expedition was launched to storm into the Red Sea and seize the port of Aden, which is situated on the Arabian Peninsula.

Despite all of the previous Portuguese victories in the open waters of the ocean, they were soundly repulsed by the galleys of Aden's defenders in the shallow waters of the Red Sea. The galleys of Saudi Arabia proved very effective in these low-lying waters. Even without any wind to blow their sails, their rowers were able to maneuver them rapidly around the Portuguese craft.

Shifting gears away from the Red Sea, the Portuguese would eventually manage to secure Hormuz on the Persian Gulf in 1515. This conquest would make the Persian Gulf a part of the Portuguese domain, with the local shah becoming an official vassal of Portugal. However, despite this success in the Persian Gulf, all repeated attempts to seize Aden would be easily swatted back by the mighty defenders of the Red Sea.

In 1514, the Portuguese sent an expedition under Jorge Álvares even farther abroad. Jorge and his compatriots ended up all the way in China, becoming the first travelers from Europe to make such a trek. The Portuguese would learn that one of the complications that they had inherited with their seizure of Malacca was the fact that the local sultan actually paid an annual tribute to the Chinese emperor.

These were matters that the Portuguese would soon have to sort out with their new Chinese neighbors in their Malaysian neighborhood. Nevertheless, the Portuguese Empire was indeed on the rise, and it would remain so for quite some time.

Chapter 8 – Toward a More Perfect Union

"When I arrive with a fleet the first thing they try to find out is how many men and what armaments we have. When they judge us invincible, they give us a good reception and trade with us in good faith. When they find us weak, they procrastinate and prepare unpredictable responses. No alliance can be established with any king or lord without military support."

-Afonso de Albuquerque

Not long after the Portuguese deposed him from Malacca, the former potentate of the region—Sultan Mahmud—appealed to the Chinese to whom he had formerly been paying an annual tribute. The response of the Chinese was lackluster at best since they felt that the loss of one measly vassal in Southeast Asia was the least of their concerns.

For centuries, China had placed its primary focus in regards to security on its northern grasslands. Ever since Genghis Khan and his Mongol horde had swooped down on China in the 13th century, the northern frontier was always of the gravest concern. Soon enough, the Portuguese would make their presence known even to the Middle Kingdom of China.

The preeminent Portuguese enforcer, Governor Afonso de Albuquerque, passed away on December 15th, 1515. He was succeeded by a man by the name of Lopo Soares de Albergaria. Albergaria was handpicked by the king of Portugal as a successor primarily because of his noble roots and his perceived loyalty. Albergaria was actually chosen to succeed Albuquerque before the prior governor had died, and he left in the spring of 1515 to replace him.

King Manuel would only learn much later of how Albuquerque had passed before Albegaria's arrival. Albergaria was indeed loyal to the Crown, but he was not quite the rugged warrior and fearless sea captain that Albuquerque had been. Even Manuel realized this. Prior to receiving word that Albuquerque was dead, he actually had second thoughts about his selection.

After Albergaria had already set sail, Manuel received word that the Mamluks were saber-rattling against Portuguese interests. Fearing that Albergaria would not be able to mount a stand against them as effectively as Albuquerque, he began to reconsider Albuquerque's removal. It was only later on that Manuel learned that Albuquerque was already dead.

Nevertheless, despite these misgivings and the big shoes he had to fill, the new governor, Albergaria, would break a lot of new ground on his own. Shortly after leaving Lisbon, Albergaria sent a delegation to Ethiopia to seek an audience with the Ethiopian emperor, who was still often perceived by the Portuguese as the legendary Christian king, Prester John.

This delegation was led by Portuguese ambassador Duarte Galvão. These forged relations would bear fruit decades later in the 1540s when a joint Portuguese/Ethiopian force successfully repulsed Islamic forces hellbent on extinguishing the Christian Ethiopian Empire from the Horn of Africa.

In the meantime, the Portuguese would lose their window of opportunity as it pertained to their crusading dream of storming the

Red Sea, taking Saudi Arabia, and then marching all the way to Jerusalem. Their old foes, the Mamluks, who had ruled from Cairo, Egypt, had been deposed by the Islamic Ottoman Empire. With its head in Istanbul (Constantinople), Turkey, the Ottomans of the 1500s were still quite a force to be reckoned with. And from 1517 onward, it would be primarily the Ottomans that the Portuguese would have to deal with as their main adversaries on the high seas.

But they certainly were not the only ones. As mentioned, the eastward expansion of the Portuguese had already reached China. It was actually that same fateful year of 1517 that a Portuguese delegation first attempted to set up official trade relations at the port of Canton, China. Initially, the Chinese were fairly friendly—if not ambivalent—when it came to the Portuguese presence.

But it would not take long for relations to break down. Exacerbating the situation was a Portuguese explorer-turned-pirate by the name of Simão de Andrade, who began to openly raid Chinese settlements on the coast. Such actions obviously would not be too endearing to the Chinese. And in 1521, the situation would erupt into a fully-fledged battle between a Portuguese fleet and Ming China.

The Portuguese were parked in China's Guangzhou harbor, attempting a rather heavy-handed approach with the Chinese to open up trade. The Chinese had had enough and sent out their most powerful ships to send the Portuguese packing. The Portuguese initially attempted to fight back, but after the Chinese unleashed a fireship, they were forced to flee.

After this exchange, the Chinese government, by imperial decree, put an official ban on all trade with the Portuguese. The ban would not be lifted until 1554. It was only a few years after this ban was lifted that the Portuguese were allowed to establish a trading post in nearby Macau. The word "allowed" is a bit of a loaded term since the Portuguese had already established an outpost on their own accord.

Even though initially, the Chinese had the Portuguese paying them "rent" (otherwise known as "custom duties") for this piece of real estate, the Portuguese would soon have complete control over all of Macau, culminating in a 1783 declaration of Macau being an official Portuguese territory. In a bizarre sense, the Portuguese could be viewed almost as squatters on Chinese territory, who, after many years, declared themselves the rightful owners! But this is basically what happened, and Macau ultimately would not be returned to China until 1999.

Taking our chronicle of Portuguese history back to the 1500s for a moment, the year 1521 was indeed a momentous one for the whole Portuguese Empire. Not only was it the year that the Portuguese were checked by China, but it also marked the passing of King Manuel. His successor to the Portuguese throne and ultimate inheritor of the Portuguese Empire was King John (João) III.

Although Manuel oversaw the greatest and most rapid expansion of Portuguese power, it literally came at a cost. And as much revenue as the spice trade brought in, Portugal was encumbered by many debts to keep its overseas empire up and running. It was this debt that King John III would have to come to grips with and carefully manage.

The population of little Portugal had grown in the meantime, and for many, the prospects of living in one of the overseas Portuguese colonies was finally starting to seem more appealing than remaining in crowded and stifling Lisbon. For most, the surest path to success was either through the clergy, the king's court, or by trying one's luck overseas. As a popular saying of the times described the state of affairs, "Those wishing to stay afloat, must choose Church, Court, or Boat."

And one of the places that the Portuguese were now frequently hopping on a boat to immigrate to was the new colony of Brazil. By 1534, Brazil had been divided into many regions, which were being settled under the leadership of the donatários, which means "endowed one." These were often noblemen who had been given a piece of territory called a donataria. Donatários were put in place to lead each of the colonial settlements in a region of Brazil that was being settled. The donatários were responsible for the well-being and security of the settlers.

To provide further security to the people in this faraway land, the position of governor-general of Brazil was established in 1549, with the role going to Tomé de Sousa. Under de Sousa, Brazil would become prosperous, and it would also become deeply involved in the slave trade.

The Portuguese had dabbled with slavery to some extent from the very beginning of their forays into West Africa. And now, there was a steady stream of African slaves (primarily from the Portuguese outpost in Angola) being brought to Brazil, in particular, to tend to sugarcane and other cash crops that were grown in the colony.

The proceeds of Brazilian sugarcane would come to be a dominant feature of the Portuguese Empire by the year 1575. Incidentally enough, all of this coincides with the establishment of the Portuguese capital of Luanda in Angola. This city was linked directly to the sugarcane market in Brazil, and it became a hub for slave trading. While all of this was going on, the nobles of Portugal began to contemplate a possible merger with Spain.

Portugal and Spain share the Iberian Peninsula, and they had long divided the spoils of extraterritorial possessions with each other. Many of the elites in both Portugal and Spain began to consider how a union of the two crowns—and the peninsula itself—might work to their benefit. This discussion then came to a head in dramatic fashion in 1578 when the king of Portugal—Sebastian I—presumedly perished during an expedition in Morocco.

Sebastian was only twenty-four years old at the time, and he had no heir. Along with forcing a desperate search for the next ruler, Sebastian had also racked up terrible debt fighting in Morocco. Whoever succeeded him would have to deal with paying for the expenses. In the immediate aftermath of his demise, the throne ultimately went to Sebastian's grand-uncle, Cardinal Henry. Yes, Henry was a Catholic priest, which perhaps makes an unusual choice for a king. But at this point, he was simply the closest in the dynastic line.

Priests, of course, are not known for marrying or having children (at least legitimate ones), so when Cardinal Harry perished just a couple of years later in January 1580, there was still no heir apparent. Instead, immediately after his passing, a board of five governors was established as an interim government to run the Portuguese Empire.

In the meantime, the grandchildren of former King Manuel I rose up as claimants. Philip II of Spain was himself a strong contender. But so was António, Prior of Crato. António was popular with many Portuguese, and although an official successor had not yet been declared, he attempted to ride his popularity all the way to the throne of Portugal. However, the five governors did not recognize him, and they held further debates on just who would ascend the throne.

Philip II initially sat on the sidelines to see if he might be selected by the panel. He was a powerful contender since, as mentioned, there was a strong faction who wished for the Iberian Union that Philip II would bring. Philip II was also already an experienced monarch in his own right.

But as the days wore on, it was clear that he was not going to easily take the throne through this board. And soon enough, Philip II grew tired of waiting for the verdict. In the end, a military force decided who the crown would go to, as Philip made the bold move to send his armies to Portugal to seize the throne by force. This led to the Battle of Alcântara on August 25th, 1580—a horrible struggle that left thousands of Portuguese dead, wounded, or captured. The casualties were not nearly as bad for the Spanish forces, who only lost around five hundred troops.

Philip II would then go on to officially assume the kingship of Portugal in 1581, establishing the long-sought-after Iberian Union. In order to smooth over the tragic bloodshed that had transpired to make this union happen, Philip granted a general amnesty to those who had challenged his quest for the Portuguese throne. It was not all bad news for the Portuguese either since Spain's massive wealth of silver (mostly mined from the Americas) was a welcome relief to Portugal's treasury, which was practically empty. Spain also sent extra military forces to Portuguese acquisitions.

Philip II was the head of a huge empire even before the union, with holdings in the Americas and the far-flung Philippines (named after Philip no less), and he was not able to remain in Portugal for long. By 1583, he had left for Madrid, where he created what was known as the council of Portugal so that he could be better kept abreast of Portuguese affairs.

In the meantime, he placed a nephew of his, Albert of Austria, in charge as a viceroy in Lisbon, Portugal. Albert turned out to be a schemer. He secretly opened up a dialogue with Queen Elizabeth I of England, a country that was at odds with Spain at the time due to the fate of the Protestant Netherlands, which Spain was desperate to bring back into the Catholic fold. The Netherlands had been fighting for its independence since 1568, and the Iberian Union had only made their struggle more frantic.

In desperate need of an ally, the Dutch had won a major coup by getting Britain on their side. Protestant England and Catholic Spain then came to blows with each other in 1588. Philip II actually attempted to invade England, but it did not turn out well for him at all. Spain ended up losing an entire armada of ships after their abortive attempt was beaten back by the English.

The emboldened English went from the defensive to the offensive, and they decided to meddle with local affairs in the Iberian Peninsula by landing in Portugal in 1589 and attempting to restore local Portuguese power. This bid failed spectacularly, but the English were much more successful in keeping the Dutch Netherlands free of Spanish interference. And ironically enough, it would be the resurgent and free Dutch who would come to haunt both the Spanish and Portuguese empires more than anything else.

Chapter 9 – Portuguese Empire under Siege

"So long as they are upheld by justice and without oppression, they are more than sufficient. But if good faith and humanity cease to be observed in these lands, then pride will overthrow the strongest walls we have. Portugal is very poor and when the poor are covetous they become oppressors. The fumes of India are powerful—I fear the time will come when instead of our present fame as warriors we may only be known as grasping tyrants."

-Afonso de Albuquerque

It has long been one of the ironies of history that although the Iberian Union was forged in the name of empowering both the Spanish and Portuguese empires, it would significantly weaken both. And it was shortly after this development that the Netherlands won its struggle against Spain, gained independence, and then went on to wallop Portuguese territories.

The Iberian Union did not bring more security to the Portuguese; rather, it helped turn them into targets of Dutch aggression. An increasingly aggressive Dutch naval power attacked the Portuguese more than the Spanish. The Dutch thought they could gain ground by stabbing the soft underbelly of imperial Portuguese holdings.

The Portuguese were spread thin, and they held their territories with a small number of troops. The Dutch would very much come to mimic the Portuguese in these tactics, but they posed a greater threat to the Portuguese than anyone else at the time since their ships and armaments were roughly on par with them. Unlike the Egyptians and Indians, whom the Portuguese larger depended on due to their faster ships and more powerful guns, the Dutch were able to match or even exceed the Portuguese in just about every fashion.

Helping to fuel the aggression and animosity between the two was the fact that the Dutch were just as fervent Protestants as the Portuguese were Catholics. The ensuing struggle between the Dutch and the Portuguese, therefore, was one of both material and religious conquest. The Portuguese came to view their Dutch adversaries with absolute contempt. As one Portuguese historian put it in 1624, "The Hollanders are merely good gunners and are otherwise fit for nothing save to be burned as desperate heretics."

The Portuguese viewed the Dutch as demented Protestants who believed in doctrinal errors, whereas the Dutch viewed the Portuguese as religious tyrants in league with a pope whom they frequently referred to as nothing short of the "antichrist." But as much as they expressed their mutual distaste over their respective belief systems, there were moments early on when the Portuguese and Dutch actually found some common ground and cooperated with each other.

When the Dutch showed up in Indonesia in 1596, for example, after a perilous voyage that killed most of their crew, the Portuguese were the ones who gave them assistance. The Portuguese already had outposts in Indonesia, and they directed the Dutch to the local ruler who would give them trading rights. But this cooperation certainly would not last long. And the first major strike by the Dutch against Portuguese possessions occurred during the years 1598 and 1599, with attacks launched on both Príncipe and São Tomé.

The Dutch tended to raid Portuguese islands and coastal enclaves that were fairly isolated and quite easy to launch hit-and-run attacks against. It would have been a much different story if the Dutch had attacked, for example, Spanish holdings in Mexico. Against a well-consolidated colony on land such as this, they would not have fared as well. But the string of settlements the Portuguese had established on isolated island chains and remote coastlines proved to be much easier targets. The Dutch would slowly graduate to taking on larger Portuguese holdings, most notably Brazil, in 1624.

In between these major strikes, the Dutch were not above engaging in piracy. Ever since the audacious seizure of the Portuguese flagship *Santa Catarina* in 1603, just about any Portuguese craft found isolated on the open waters was fair game in the minds of the Dutch. Ironically enough, the Dutch essentially began treating the Portuguese in a strikingly similar, ruthless manner as the Portuguese had treated most Muslim-based ships in the previous century.

Just as the Portuguese typically considered it fair game to seize the ships of Muslim merchants in the Indian Ocean for no other reason than disdain of their religious faith, the Protestant Dutch were now essentially doing the same thing to the Portuguese due to their disdain of Catholicism.

Just a couple of years after the seizure of *Santa Catarina*, two integral Spice Islands—Tidore and Ambon—were taken by the Dutch in 1605. The Portuguese, of course, were not completely defenseless against this onslaught, and they fought back as vigorously as they could. At times, they were quite successful in repulsing the Dutch advances. This was the case in 1622 when they easily pushed back the Dutch who were attempting to invade Macau.

After they were beaten back by the Portuguese, the Dutch then had the audacity to raid the Chinese coastal city of Fujian before issuing demands to the Chinese to cease trading with the Iberian Peninsula. China was slow to answer, but a couple of years later, it did—and in a big way. The Chinese sent out a large army of tens of thousands of men, which successfully expelled the Dutch from their holdings in nearby Taiwan.

That same year, the Portuguese lost their outpost on the Persian Gulf. This was not due to Dutch interference but rather the English. The English had also begun operating in the region, and due to their technical assistance with artillery, the Persian forces were able to finally expel the Portuguese from their midst.

Soon, though, the English became increasingly alarmed at the progress of the Dutch, and they soon began to change course. They went from an ambivalent to somewhat hostile tact toward the Portuguese to engaging in diplomatic relations. The two forged a basic alliance, which led to the Anglo-Portuguese Truce of 1635.

As much trouble as the Dutch were causing the Portuguese in Asia, their efforts to hamper Portugal's African settlements were much less successful. Several efforts—including two swipes at Mozambique—were repulsed until the Dutch finally decided to simply establish a settlement of their own, which they did in 1652 at the Cape of Good Hope.

The Dutch would be pigeonholed in this meager outpost for quite some time, almost like they were in some sort of colonial quarantine, while the Portuguese continued to expand their landholdings in Africa during this period. The Dutch were a little more successful in their efforts to pressure Portuguese holdings in Angola. In August of 1648, they managed to establish alliances with both the king of Kongo and the queen of neighboring Jagas. With this coalition, the Dutch drove the Portuguese into toeholds in the Kwanza Valley.

However, they were able to regroup, and with the help of auxiliary forces shipped in from Brazil, they were quickly able to retake the Angolan capital of Luanda, followed by the rest of Angola itself. The end of hostilities between the Dutch and the Portuguese was then in sight, and an official peace treaty was signed between the two parties in 1663. That very same year, the Iberian Union, which for nearly one hundred years had bound the fate of Spain and Portugal together, finally came undone.

Upon Portugal's renewed independence, her empire—particularly Portuguese holdings in Asia—had shrunk considerably. Portuguese India was down to the merest of toeholds. This fact was duly noted by a Jesuit priest by the name of Padre Manuel Godinho that same fateful year of 1663.

Padre Manuel had traveled from India to the Persian Gulf and then back to Portugal, reporting, "The Lusitanian Indian Empire or State, which formerly dominated the whole of the East, and comprised eight thousand leagues of sovereignty, including twenty-nine provincial capital cities as well as many others of lesser note, and which gave the law to thirty-three tributary kingdoms, amazing the whole world with its vast extent, stupendous victories, thriving trade and immense riches, is now either through its own sins or else through the inevitable decay of great empires, reduced to so few lands and cities that one may well doubt whether that state was smaller in its very beginning than it is now at its end."

Yes, by the time Portugal had regained mastery of its own destiny, the Portuguese Empire had indeed contracted considerably. From here on out, despite a few toeholds in Asia, the heart and soul of the Portuguese Empire would be primarily in South America and Africa.

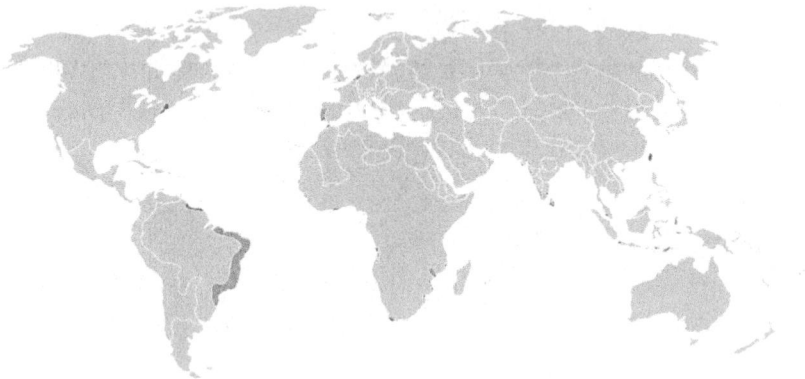

What the Portuguese (green) and Dutch (blue) holdings looked like after the Dutch-Portuguese War.

https://commons.wikimedia.org/wiki/File:DutchPortugueseWar1661.png

Initially, the major export from Portugal's Brazilian holdings in South America was its namesake, brazilwood. But the land would prove to be much more profitable than that. In 1693, both gold and diamonds were located in the region of Minas Gerais. This Brazilian gold rush brought in a large number of immigrants, and this part of Brazil became alive with activity. Due to these developments, and combined with losses in Asia, Brazil became the main hub of imperial Portugal.

Around that very same time, the Portuguese were also looking for gold and other precious resources in their holdings in southeastern Africa. These efforts led them to expand their territory farther west, with the ultimate dream of linking their colony in Mozambique on Africa's eastern coast all the way to Angola on Africa's western coast.

Their efforts, however, were hampered by a local Bantu chief called Changamire, who rose up to lead a resistance against Portuguese expansion. Changamire would continue to stand up to the Portuguese until his death in 1695. After this powerful chief's death, the Bantu once again became too divided among themselves to pose much of a threat to the Portuguese.

During this time of resurgence, there were many notable Portuguese who would attempt to distinguish themselves. Among them was a member of the famous da Gama family—João da Maia da Gama. João da Maia da Gama was born in 1673, so he was separated from his famous relative and Portuguese pioneer, Vasco da Gama, by a couple of centuries. In 1692, as a young man, he headed for what remained of the Portuguese outposts in India. By 1693, he was in Goa, and he was soon taking part in naval battles against English ships, which had aligned themselves with forces from Omani Sultanate.

João ended up fighting off and on in the Persian Gulf over the next few years before heading back to Portugal, arriving back home in 1699. After returning to Portugal, da Gama fought in the War of the Spanish Succession, which had a direct impact on the Portuguese. He also assisted in the destruction of a naval blockade of the Straits of

Gibraltar, which had been carried out courtesy of the French in the year 1705.

A few years later, in 1708, da Gama arrived in Brazil, where he was made the governor of the Brazilian region of Paraíba from 1708 to 1717 and then governor of Maranhão e Grão-Pará from 1722 to 1728. Perhaps proving his relations to the great explorer Vasco da Gama, on the heels of João da Maia da Gama's governorship of Maranhão, he went on an exhausting expedition from Maranhão all the way to Pernambuco.

It was a trip that would take up most of the year 1729. In 1730, Pernambuco had been taken by the Dutch, and the Portuguese settlers there would remain under Dutch rule for decades. In the end, the settlers themselves decided to cast off the yoke of Dutch oppression, rising up against the usurpers in 1745.

It was a long and protracted struggle, but by 1754, Pernambuco was once again part of Portuguese Brazil. However, it would take nearly ten years for the Dutch to acknowledge this fact, doing so only in 1761. This would come to serve the Portuguese Empire well since Brazil would someday become a fallback position when Portugal itself came to be threatened.

Chapter 10 – The Age of Pombal and Beyond

"The cultivation of literary pursuits forms the basis of all sciences, and in their perfection consist the reputation and prosperity of kingdoms."

-Sebastião José de Carvalho e Mello (Pombal)

By the 1750s, the Portuguese Empire had entered into the so-called "Age of Pombal." It is called this because the entire age was named after one of the most powerful and influential figures in Portuguese history—Sebastião José de Carvalho e Melo, 1ˢᵗ Marquis of Pombal. It is from this title that we get his more widely known moniker of "Pombal."

Sebastião, better known as Pombal, began life in relative obscurity. His family did have some connections to the nobility, but it was lacking in scope. After his father abruptly perished when Pombal was twenty-one years old, the chance for his own upward mobility seemed grim. Pombal managed to marry into a more prosperous family, as he wed the niece of the count of Arcos. However, it should be noted that most of her household was against the match.

Nevertheless, this union brought much more clout to Pombal, and from here on out, he was able to slowly rise up the ranks. In 1739, he became the ambassador to Britain, and in 1745, he was made ambassador to Vienna, where he stayed until 1749. In both of these postings, Pombal became acutely aware that the Portuguese Empire was increasingly behind its European rivals in almost every sphere.

He marveled at the technological innovations taking place in Britain and the strong bureaucracy that had been established in Vienna, which was, in those days, the seat of the Holy Roman Empire. During his foray at Vienna, Pombal's wife passed. Pombal didn't hesitate to find a new bride, and once again, he chose a woman of high birth, the daughter of an Austrian count no less—Eleonora Ernestina von Daun.

Eleonora was actually the lady-in-waiting for the Holy Roman empress. This brought Pombal right to the top echelons of European nobility. Incidentally enough, the king of Portugal, John (João) V, was actually married to a Viennese noble, Maria Anna, who is sometimes dubbed the "Austrian Queen." Pombal's wife was on close terms with Maria Anna, and it was through this connection that Pombal was able to secure a transfer back to the Portuguese court in 1749.

Pombal was now a veteran politician. He was well connected to high-ranking officials both at home and abroad. Back in Portugal, his first objective was to catch the Portuguese Empire up in the areas Pombal felt were seriously lagging. At the king's court, Pombal pushed for many initiatives in an attempt to jumpstart the Portuguese Empire and make it better equipped to deal with the most pressing matters of the 18th century.

Pombal's chance to really make a difference came in 1750 when King Joseph (José; his father died in late July 1750) made him his secretary of state for foreign affairs and war. It was at this point that the Portuguese Empire entered into the so-called "Pombal Age," and it would last for several decades.

The first major incident that occurred during Pombal's tenure was the tremendous earthquake that erupted in the Portuguese capital of Lisbon on November 1st, 1755. To say that this earthquake was incredibly destructive would not be an understatement. The quake is believed to have clocked in at around nine on the Richter scale. Just to give some reference, the only known earthquake to have been larger was the one that hit Chile in 1960, which was recorded at a record 9.5 on the Richter scale. This earthquake affected all of Portugal, and the initial tremors were immediately followed by a couple of terribly devastating aftershocks.

Several major towns in Portugal were literally leveled to the ground. In the immediate aftermath, it was quite clear that Portugal—the seat of the Portuguese Empire—was in a state of emergency. It was something akin to what Rome must have been like after it burned, and Nero was blamed for fiddling too much. However, the devastation that was wreaked upon Portugal was far greater than what Rome experienced.

The earthquake was followed by many fires, which was largely attributed to the fact that the quake happened on All Saints' Day. All Saints' Day is a day of reverence of the saints. On this day, Catholic believers light a multitude of candles. It has been widely theorized that the earthquake knocked down many of the candlelit altars, which resulted in numerous outbreaks of fire.

It has been said that after it was all over with, about 90 percent of the residences in Lisbon alone were no longer suitable for human habitation. One can only imagine the survivors literally clawing their way out of the burned-out rubble only to find themselves homeless and left to wander the ruined landscape of the city. This terrible situation would prove to be just the kind of apocalyptic climate in which a form of martial law and a would-be dictator might emerge.

And that was basically the framework that Pombal found himself working under. However, not all was lost; the king had survived, mainly due to the sheer coincidence that he and his family were away at a country resort far from the epicenter of Lisbon. Yet, upon the king's return, Pombal was the one who took on a leading role in advising the king, famously instructing the worried monarch to "Bury the dead and care for the living."

In other words, despite the devastation, King Joseph was informed it would be best just to cut their losses as quickly as possible and simply move on. The dead were already gone; it was time to focus on the future of those who had survived. Such advice perhaps is lacking in sentimentality, but on a logical level, it is sound enough. The Portuguese Empire needed to rebuild and move on, lest one of their enemies should somehow try and use their current hardship against them.

Seeing Pombal as an indispensable executive in this crisis, he was given great authority to ensure that order was established in the chaos. Just as he had described, Pombal directed the burying of the dead and then moved on to look after the living. The death toll was so high and the burden of finding a final resting place so enormous that the vast majority of the deceased were simply given a burial at sea—a more polite way of saying that they were systematically disposed of by dropping them into the ocean.

As for the living, Pombal enacted programs that would give survivors a temporary roof over their heads. He also saw to it that anyone dastardly enough to loot through the ruined hovels would be prosecuted. He posted Portuguese troops on every corner and authorized them to put a stop to any unauthorized rummaging through the wreckage. In Pombal's mind, it would all be sorted out in due time but only in an orderly fashion under his direction. There would be no wanton looting in the streets.

In yet another parallel to when Rome burned, giving Emperor Nero the excuse to build brand new buildings, Pombal seized the same opportunity. He realized that the leveling of Lisbon allowed him to finally embark upon his great dream of modernizing the capital of the Portuguese Empire. Aiding in this was the fact that the spooked king—Joseph I—decided he did not want to rebuild his ruined palace.

This cleared the way for Pombal to erect a modernized administrative center instead. These subtle moves away from the monarchy translated into many other ruined buildings and locales being transformed as well. The Palace Square, for example, was rechristened as the Square of Commerce. In all of these renovations, it was clear that the monarchy had been diminished and that businesses had risen to prominence instead.

In the rebuilding of the capital, Pombal relied upon military engineers to construct sturdy and stable infrastructure. The care with which this was done is evident, as all of the new residences were erected upon a well-planned grid. Each building was created with an earthquake-resistant inner frame, as well as a cistern.

Pombal wanted to make sure that these many upgrades would not be forgotten. He wanted future generations to be able to continue to make these kinds of improvements. It was with this intention in mind that, in 1756, Pombal established a school of architecture.

After rebuilding Portugal's infrastructure, Pombal sought to rebuild the general economy of the Portuguese Empire. And a big part of that was done through better streamlining how Portugal conducted trade. At this point in time, the British were the most dominant in overseas commerce. However, Britain was an ally, so any competition had to be done in a manner that would not provoke the British. This prompted the so-called "Pombaline plan" of monopolies. This plan revolved around the creation of independent companies that could work as autonomous monopolies.

One of the most successful of these companies was the Grão Pará and Maranhão Company, which was given a twenty-year monopoly over all trade conducted in the Amazonian sector of Brazil. This company worked on weeding out independent Portuguese traders who were cutting deals with British merchants in favor of individual profit over the general well-being of the Portuguese Empire's economy.

The plan worked well enough, and these internal developments seemed to go under the radar as far as Britain was concerned. Further streamlining the control of economic trade was the establishment of a national treasury for all imperial revenue and expenditures, which was established in 1761. This development allowed all profits to be directed to this one official repository.

But this state of affairs came under scrutiny in 1762 after Portugal was drawn into the Seven Years' War. Portugal had initially remained neutral, but after Portugal's refusal to stop trade with Britain, Spanish soldiers declared war on the Portuguese Empire. Portugal turned to its ally, Great Britain, and the Spanish troops were ultimately repulsed. Portugal managed to come out on the winning side of the conflict.

However, the close operations between Britain and Portugal had made Britain better aware of Portugal's trade strategy with its monopolized companies. Britain did not like what it saw and ordered the Portuguese to ensure fairer trade.

Pombal, in the meantime, had begun a real reign of terror both at home and abroad. In Brazil, the Jesuits were viewed with the utmost suspicion over Pombal's accusations that they were not following protocol. He also claimed that they were hoarding money. Pombal circulated many anti-Jesuit tracts during his reign, and much of the subsequent Portuguese rancor against the Jesuit order dates back to these actions during the Pombal Age.

Pombal also persecuted any and everyone who he felt to be somehow disloyal to him or the Portuguese Empire. Many of these were locked up on obscure charges and held indefinitely. One of Pombal's biggest purges occurred back in 1758 when an assassination attempt was made on the king of Portugal. The king was actually visiting his mistress, Teresa Leonor de Távora, when his entourage was ambushed.

The king received two minor gunshot wounds but was quickly on the mend. Pombal, however, was ready to go to war. He arrested not only the king's mistress but also nearly everyone associated with her, including about a dozen Jesuits for reasons only entirely known to Pombal. Pombal stated that he thought they plotted to overthrow the monarchy.

Pombal took the plot against the king personally, and many historians believe that there is good reason for him to have done so. Just prior to this attempt on the king's life, several nobles had met with him and attempted to convince the king to get rid of Pombal. The nobles did not like Pombal's policies, and they requested that the king remove him from office. It is believed that after the king refused to listen to their pleas, the nobles entered into a conspiracy to get rid of the king instead. Getting rid of the king, after all, would get rid of Pombal.

If this were indeed the case, it is really no wonder that Pombal—a vindictive enough character as it is—would have gone to such extreme lengths to destroy those who had sought to do him harm. But his ability to pursue his opponents would only last as long as he was in power. It is said that by the time of King Joseph's death in 1777 and Pombal's oust from power, around eight hundred souls were finally set free from their bonds.

Upon taking the reins from her deceased father, Queen Dona Maria I ordered the release of all of Pombal's political prisoners. Shortly thereafter, Pombal sent the queen his official resignation. Many of those who gained their release with the ascension of Queen Dona Maria were itching for revenge against Pombal and urged the queen to go further and hold Pombal criminally accountable for his actions.

But any such attempt to follow this course invariably led to a dead end since all of Pombal's actions had been co-signed by the deceased king. And since Queen Dona Maria was not about to convict her late father along with Pombal, she was forced to just quietly put both Pombal and the whole Pombal Age to the side.

After the end of Pombaline Portugal, the Portuguese Empire began its long march of decline. The first indication that the empire was beginning to fall apart at the seams occurred in 1789 when Minas Gerais, a profitable province of Brazil, began asserting itself as an independent state. However, this bid for independence did not last long, and its ring leaders were quickly rounded up and arrested. But this was just the first of several revolts that would rise up throughout the next few decades.

The real game-changer came after the French Revolution and the subsequent rise of Napoleonic France. Napoleon would threaten Portugal and the Iberian Peninsula as a whole, and the entire Portuguese royal court was forced to evacuate to Brazil in 1808. This led to the 1815 declaration of the United Kingdom of Portugal, Brazil and the Algarves, in which Brazil's Rio de Janeiro rather than Portugal's Lisbon became the capital of the Portuguese Empire.

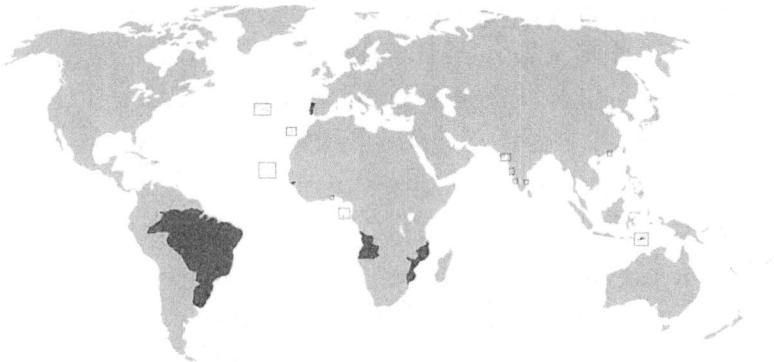

The United Kingdom of Portugal, Brazil and the Algarves.

The royal court would eventually make its way back to Portugal in 1821, but the previous shift in power had emboldened Brazil to vie for its own independence. This independence was declared on September 7th, 1822, with surprisingly little resistance from the Portuguese Crown. The remnants of the Portuguese Empire would then refocus its interests almost solely on Africa.

The two jewels left in Portugal's crown were now Angola on the west side of Africa and Mozambique on the east side. In between these two was a whole corridor of unclaimed territory. By the late 1880s, when the so-called "Scramble for Africa" was in full force, the Portuguese dreamed of finally connecting these two Portuguese colonies together.

The British, who sought to link up their holdings in Egypt to their territory in South Africa, did not approve of this venture, and they did everything they could to prevent it. This led to the British Ultimatum of 1890, in which the British issued direct demands to King Carlos I of Portugal (r. 1889-1908) to cease and desist with any further attempts to link up the two colonies. The fact that the Portuguese king was so easily cowed by the British was not forgotten by his Portuguese detractors, and it would ultimately lead to his death.

King Carlos was assassinated by his critics on February 1st, 1908. A few years later, in 1914, World War One broke out. What remained of the Portuguese Empire would face even more dire challenges with the rise of German aggression. During the war, the Germans sought to seize Angola from the Portuguese. Repeated acts of aggression led to Portugal's entry into the war against Germany in 1916.

Along with supplying troops to the Western Front, Portugal was on the frontlines of submarine warfare, along with the British, in and around their colonial possessions of Angola and Mozambique. Portugal came out on the winning side of this war and was able to keep its colonial possessions, but it was just a matter of time before these colonies would seek independence on their own.

The first big push for the Portuguese to decolonize their overseas possessions occurred in the aftermath of World War Two. In the late 1940s, Portugal was being pressured to rid itself of its last footholds in India. The Portuguese leader at the time—strongman António de Oliveira Salazar—refused, citing the holdings as being essential to the welfare of Portugal.

Nevertheless, in 1954, Portugal lost two of its outposts due to local insurrections, and in 1961, the Indian military unilaterally seized and dismantled the final Portuguese settlement in India. During that same fateful year, Angola also rose up to shake itself out of Portugal's grip. This was followed by similar uprisings in Guinea in 1963 and Mozambique in 1964, with the former gaining independence in 1974 and the latter formally gaining independence in 1975.

After the Portuguese possessions in Africa freed themselves, the next to declare independence was East Timor in Southeast Asia in 1975. The last vestige of what had been the Portuguese Empire, the old trading outpost in Macau, was handed over to China on December 20th, 1999. It was this final release of overseas territory that finalized the complete and utter dissolution of what had been one of the greatest empires the world has ever known.

Conclusion: The Pride of the Portuguese

The rise of the Portuguese Empire was quite an unexpected and incredible feat. The tiny nation of Portugal was carved out of the Iberian Peninsula after Islamic armies subdued almost all of the peninsula. Once the Reconquista had run its course, Portugal proper rose to prominence as a small but determined country, perched right on the Atlantic seaboard.

It was from this little perch that the Portuguese sailed forth into the unknown to find both new routes as well as new lands. Expeditions were commissioned by the Portuguese monarch to round the tip of Africa. Bartolomeu Dias succeeded in this mission and literally charted the course for those who would follow. This paved the way for explorers and conquerors like Vasco da Gama to solidify these gains for the Portuguese Empire.

As for those who bore witness to the arrival of these foreign explorers, the initial reaction was one of astonishment. The fact that the Portuguese could travel such a great distance seemed nothing short of a miracle. And when the strangers proclaimed that it was "Christians and spices" that they were after, it struck those who heard it as both incredible and incredulous.

But these were indeed the primary motivators of the Portuguese voyages to India. Ever since the fall of Constantinople in 1453, the overland routes had been largely blocked off, and the merchants of the Islamic world had a monopoly over the Indian spice trade, ferrying goods from India to Saudi Arabia and Egypt, then overcharging the Venetian middlemen who dealt with them at sky-rocketing rates.

The Portuguese sought to cut out these middlemen once and for all by going directly to the source of this great wealth of trade goods. This not only altered the entire state of the global economy but also opened up new lands for exploration. Soon, Portugal would have an empire that spanned the Americas, Africa, India, and Southeast Asia. Portugal was on top of the world, but from here on out, it was just a slow and steady decline.

Spain attempted to merge with the Portuguese Empire, and then the Dutch attempted to supplant them. Portugal was greatly weakened by the 18th and 19th centuries, but it continued to hang on. It was not until the aftermath of the two world wars that the local residents of Portugal's imperial holdings began to become vocal about the chances of their own independence.

Even then, however, Portuguese strongman António de Oliveira Salazar tried to hang on, but the die had already been cast. By 1999, with the handover of Macau to China, it was at its end. Nevertheless, the sheer audacity of little Portugal's endeavors is still a point of pride with many Portuguese since it reveals an ingenious and indomitable spirit that continues to live on.

Here's another book by Captivating History that you might like

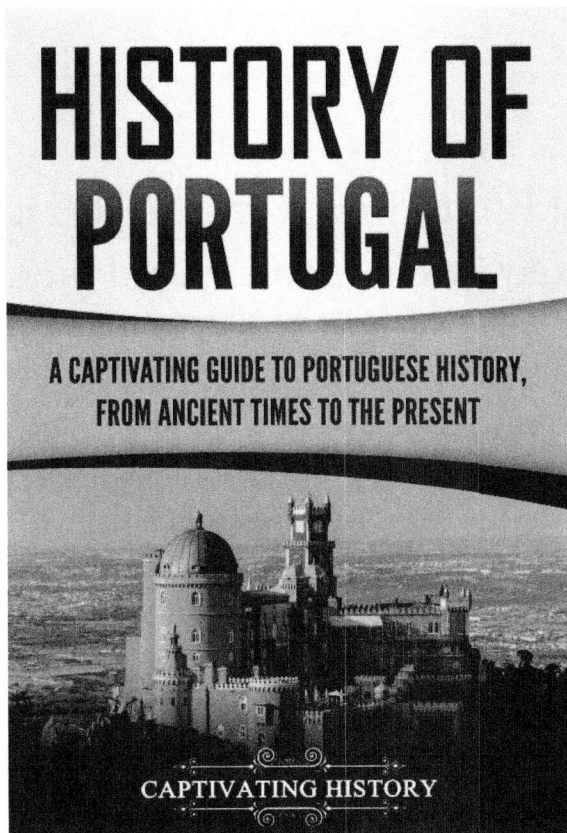

Free Bonus from Captivating History
(Available for a Limited time)

Hi History Lovers!

Now you have a chance to join our exclusive history list so you can get your first history ebook for free as well as discounts and a potential to get more history books for free! Simply visit the link below to join.

Captivatinghistory.com/ebook

Also, make sure to follow us on Facebook, Twitter and Youtube by searching for Captivating History.

Appendix A: Further Reading and Reference

Conquerors: How Portugal Forged the First Global Empire. Roger Crowley. 2015.

A History of Portugal and the Portuguese Empire, Vol 2. A. R. Disney. 2007.

The Portuguese Seaborne Empire: 1415-1825. C. R. Boxer. 1969.

A History of Modern Ethiopia. Bahru Zewde. 2001.

Printed in Great Britain
by Amazon